The Yo(u)niverse Paradox

Revealing the Mystery of You

John Ferris

BALBOA.
PRESS

A DIVISION OF HAY HOUSE

Balboa Press books may be ordered through booksellers or by contacting:

Balboa Press
A Division of Hay House
1663 Liberty Drive
Bloomington, IN 47403
www.balboapress.com
1 (877) 407-4847

Because of the dynamic nature of the Internet, any web addresses or links contained in this book may have changed since publication and may no longer be valid. The views expressed in this work are solely those of the author and do not necessarily reflect the views of the publisher, and the publisher hereby disclaims any responsibility for them.

The author of this book does not dispense medical advice or prescribe the use of any technique as a form of treatment for physical, emotional, or medical problems without the advice of a physician, either directly or indirectly. The intent of the author is only to offer information of a general nature to help you in your quest for emotional and spiritual well-being. In the event you use any of the information in this book for yourself, which is your constitutional right, the author and the publisher assume no responsibility for your actions.

Any people depicted in stock imagery provided by Thinkstock are models, and such images are being used for illustrative purposes only. Certain stock imagery © Thinkstock.

Author photo by: Peter Bennett Photography

Print information available on the last page.

ISBN: 978-1-5043-5915-3 (sc)
ISBN: 978-1-5043-5932-0 (e)

Balboa Press rev. date: 06/16/2016

DEDICATION

I dedicate this book to my son Jordan for the strength to move forward. To the love and support of my wife Karen throughout the most challenging of circumstances and to my beautiful daughter Robyn for the inspiration to discover life is eternal and we are never truly apart.

FOREWORD

This book came to be written by John as a result of his search for a plausible, fundamentally sound, intellectually challenging, scientifically acceptable and personally enhancing explanation for the human existence.

And it's indeed a pleasure to try and set the scene to John's efforts to "Join up the Dots" and in so doing, inform the thirsty reader about the meaning of life.

As an obstetrician I am well aware that we, the human race, are still struggling over the "when" it all begins, never mind ends. Or if indeed it does either or neither, as John may contend.

Does life begin when the sperm enters the egg? Or when the multiplying mitotic outcome of that encounter burrows and implants into the mother's womb? Or when the resultant embryo develops a beating heart about four weeks later? Or when the foetus reaches 24 weeks gestation? Or when birth occurs? Or when the first breath of air is taken? These questions alone daily challenge medics, lawyers, ethicists, clerics and the laity, and yet there is no consensus.

Life outside the mother's womb here on earth can be thought of as mirroring the nine months that precedes it. A period of three months development as an embryo parallels the years as a child and adolescent. There is then a period of physical and intellectual growth in both the pre and post birth states, and this is then finally followed by preparation for birth for the foetus, and death for the ageing adult. So, taking that analogy, there are at least two lives lived by the time the earthly heart stops beating. The life before life, the life after birth until "death", but then? The great unknown. A third "life?"

And of course humanly perceived tragedy can prematurely occur in either of the first two scenarios. Birth and death at what we believe is the "right time" is normally an uplifting and reflective time. A birth of a live healthy infant at term is a joy for all, while the death of a loved one who has truly had their time and run their race can also be a blessed time.

John and his devoted and fully supportive wife Karen have been on an intriguing journey since the, all would say, terribly untimely loss from this world of their daughter Robyn who was afflicted with an incurable brain tumour at the age of seven years. The sort of situation exactly that convinced Stephen

Fry, in recent conversation with the Irish TV presenter Gay Byrne, to say that he wanted no truck with a God that allowed such an occurrence. John struggled with the two available options that were presented to him as solutions within the coping mechanism traditionally available in his environs. "Glorious Eternal Life" or "The End".

So, is there a third life for us all? Is it inevitable? Is the good place, heaven, just for those who have lived a "clean" life? Is it dependant on a pre death declaration being made for a particular man made religion? Are there grades of afterlife? Is there a special place for non believers? Or does it just end? Dust to dust?

Or is there a perhaps much more believable explanation that embraces scientific thinking, spirituality, metaphysics and logic and is quite simply, just fact.....the way it is. No decisions to make. No human input required.

John has been meditating, thinking, reading, learning, discussing, and becoming increasingly sure that he has, at last, got the dots joined up and can inform us all of what the third "life", and indeed the first and second lives, are all about. It's all a continuum. It's all a paradox!

I think it's fair to say he believes he has "cracked it". John trusts that having read his text, you too will have become enlightened, and similarly reassured that it's not over when you think it's over.

I do hope you find this book thought provoking, and perhaps, who knows, life changing. Meanwhile, I think I might have to read it again, and again, and again!

Prof Jim Dornan MD(Hons) FRCOG FRCPI
Chair Health & Life Sciences UU
Chair Fetal Medicine QUB (rtd)
Author of An Everyday Miracle

CONTENTS

INTRODUCTION

My story of awakening

Where has Robyn gone? Will I ever see her again? These were the questions I asked myself on the worst day of my life. Writing these words brings the unbelievable pain back. I'm not the first and certainly won't be the last to feel pain so intensely that you feel your heart is being squeezed and twisted so tightly into the tiniest knot imaginable with the feeling that it's ready to explode into a searing inferno.

Mainstream science believes the Big Bang originated from an infinitesimally small point, compressed so tightly and comprising all the energy of the universe - known as the singularity - which exploded so violently with such energy that it created everything.

I believe each of us at the core of our being, centred within the heart, contains a singularity. The singularity is fundamental to all existence. The singularity is not only the connector of your soul to every other soul, but the whole soul itself. It is the seat of conscious awareness that holds within it absolutely everything whilst at the same time is also the expression of all. It is the puppeteer without the strings. Your soul has a sole purpose, to experience whatever you choose. Your soul is connected to every other soul within what could be termed the over soul or, from our point of view, the universal soul that springs forth from the perception of the Big Bang singularity and beyond. This soul system evolves and can be best understood when it is viewed holographically in a fractal nature from our point of view. It is an eternal dance to infinity and beyond.

My intent for writing this book is twofold. It is the culmination of seven years of seeking the truth. I have realised that there is no "the truth" there is only "your truth", which takes place within overarching unifying principles (laws) which orchestrate the entire symphony. This is ultimate reality. Sounds like a paradox?.......It is! Put another way, each of us constructs a reality model with the stories we tell ourselves that all overlap subject to specific universal laws. Does that suggest an intelligent designer? It would appear to, but the question is "who or what is doing the design and for what purpose?" Paradoxes exist everywhere. This is why, we the human race, can never resolve anything. Sounds pathetic really but it is by design and when we as a human race can accept this, then and only then can progress be made. Paradoxically paradoxes are closed loop systems with open loop evolution. If life was straightforward, rational and always based on logic the psychological drama we play out on a daily basis would have been resolved long ago and rendered meaningless and boring. We are creators each and every one of us. My aim is to open up your mind to this prospect and for you to grapple with and ultimately know the fundamental level of existence and the purpose of it all.

> "Know the truth and the truth shall make you free"
>
> -Jesus of Nazareth

Before some of you close the book thinking this is another religious doctrine to be followed it most certainly is not, quite the opposite really. I consider myself a spiritual being, not religious or atheist, or a believer that science has all the answers. By spiritual I mean that I believe all things and all-non-things come from a single source which is whole and complete and is the connector of all things and all non-things. In other words the variety of life springs from one essence and you are eternally woven within that essence with free will to choose whatever you decide. The trick is, from all the possibilities available, to not choose limiting beliefs i.e. to believe science has all the answers or a certain religion can explain everything. An approach that excludes anything cannot claim to explain everything. Make choices that not only serve you but others also, keep it inclusive. Give and you shall receive, like much that is contained within the bible is not a religious term, it is spiritual, unlimited and without boundaries.

At the conception of my awakening I felt I had to look at the whole picture, not find a tunnel of comfort and just burrow into it ignoring the rest. To answer my questions I wanted to know what religion had to say and not just Christianity. I wanted to know what science had to say, what answers the paranormal had and the meaning of spirituality. I also was sub-consciously aware that to understand this whole picture I needed to get to grips with the fundamental principles of how things work. What the governing forces are. I likened it to a master jigsaw puzzle, putting it together piece by piece. I came to see the patterns of existence - self repeating patterns that appeared to connect everything.

Secondly this book is written for you in the hope that it will inspire a broader outlook in life and by the realisation that it is you who constructs the prison walls that you experience your life within and it is you, and only you, who can tear down these walls.

I am writing this book after seven years of searching. Ironically seven would appear to be a spiritually significant number. In psychological circles it is considered that at seven years old your ego is fully active, at fourteen you go through puberty. At twenty one you come of age, whilst twenty eight is considered your physical peak. At thirty five your mental faculties are maximised and at forty two your spirit awakens within. Of course there are no fixed boundaries but this cycle would appear to be statistically significant. My spiritual awakening began in my forty second year. My daughter, my inspiration, was seven.

In the hours, days, weeks, months and even years after my daughter's crossing over I touched the singularity within my heart again and again and again. Every time the pain I brought to it was relieved by the awareness that life was more than I believed it to be, was bigger, was larger, was greater, was eternal. From that day forth my Spiritual journey began. I use the term spiritual because I see it as the best label I can associate it with. Spirituality to me is all about questioning with an open mind. Questions, questions, questions! It felt like a constant personal inquisition. I would read book after book after book. All the time asking myself questions. Sometimes I would converse with others, my wife in particular, who obviously was going through the same emotional drama as myself. But mostly it was an internal journey of inquiry and insights. The insights would arrive in the most random of ways. I might wake up in the middle of the night and an answer would pop into my head, or it could be contained within a dream or might even be on a passing billboard. The answers to my questions came to me through what I would later recognise as synchronicity.

Synchronicity can be viewed as meaningful coincidence brought about by you. It was Carl Jung who first coined the phrase synchronicity. A few months after Robyn set off on her new journey my wife Karen, son Jordan and myself were very kindly invited by Billy McCrory of "Shine-a-Light", a local charitable organisation which helps children and their families cope with child illnesses to get away for a week's break. We accepted and prior to departing I asked Robyn to give me a sign that she will be with us on our trip. I felt confident but still pleasantly surprised when the minibus taking us from where we had parked our car to the airport had a name printed on the side. Apart from the fact that buses tend not to have names, to discover the bus was named Robyn, instilled within me the faith of synchronistic events and their power.

Intuitively from the outset I knew it was not about looking outside, it was about going within. I had no idea why, it was more a feeling. To achieve the level of understanding that I was seeking the answers must be at the fundamental level. This sounds obvious now, but the way we are conditioned in western society we tend to observe outwardly to attain the answers. Initially this appears very fruitful. We travel down paths which provide amazing insights only to hit blockages along the way which tend to produce more questions than answers. At these junctures artistic licence takes over and we develop incredible stories to attempt to explain away any problematic situation. Years pass, quite often decades until technology catches up with the theories and then the magic happens. The new technology appears to confirm the original theory (at this point I can sense many people verbalising, "What an idiot! That's the way it works dummy!!!")…….. But then the next bottleneck appears and another drama evolves. The final piece always appears within touching distance, but eternally out of reach. When merging spiritual wisdom with scientific advances a clearer yet foggier picture appears (calm down it's paradoxical). 'Seek and ye shall find' is built into the system. When you come to terms with this deeper spiritual significance the puzzle not only unravels it simultaneously pieces together.

In today's society it is my belief we give our power away much too easily. I would imagine if we did a survey on which group of people have the most knowledge about life's biggest questions, "Who am I? Where do I come from? What is the purpose of life? Does God exist?" it would be a close call between the scientific community and religious leaders. The battle between science and religion still rages to this day, thankfully without the killing. My belief is that the answer lies in the middle ground between the two. At the centre, the core of life, lies spirituality. I aim to define what spirituality really is and how it permeates throughout your whole existence hiding in the shadows ready at any moment to reveal itself as your true nature.

Life itself is paradoxical, there is no absolute right or wrong. Everything arises from your point of view and that point of view is where your power resides. Everything in the universe has a polar opposite which is a twofold process based on the power of three. My aim, for those not yet aware of this, is to provide a compelling argument in favour of seeing the world through new eyes.

> "When you make the two into one, and when you make the inner as the outer, and the upper as the lower, and when you make the male and female into a single one, so that the male shall not be male, and the female shall not be female......then you will enter [the Kingdom of heaven]."

> -Jesus (the gnostic gospels)

The male and female is referencing the opposites of masculine and feminine not biological gender. Creation evolves from one whole entity. There is nothing in existence that this entity is not. Everything originates from this oneness, you can call this God, Wholeness, Source, Spirit, Infinity, All that is. It is difficult to express linguistically something that cannot be boxed. For anything to be defined as something it must appear as a separate object to a subjective observer. This process is known as duality, what we term the Mind!

How does this oneness become two? By dividing itself into two with both parts or more accurately activities having the ability to reflect back on the whole. By default this process becomes three; to have two activities you must also have the space in-between which creates the illusion of separation. This I believe is how mind comes into being. It operates as a feedback loop with the law of opposites based on the power of three for the 'soul' purpose of having a benchmark to attribute meaning. By taking a quantum leap the whole can divide itself up infinitely (the many) with each individuation being able to reflect back on all the magnificence of the whole (the one). In other words, the whole becomes many activities or "points of view" with each always being eternally connected to the whole. For this to occur we require the illusion of the space in between which is the connector of all things. So what we have is the Whole, the point of view and the illusory space in between. The power of three: The Wholly Trinity.

The illusion of space allows you to create a playground to tell your story about your objective experiences, in which you feed back to the source your personal thoughts and feelings about your narrative. You co-create your reality with this source.

A human being is part of a whole, called by us the universe, a part limited In time and space. He experiences himself, his thoughts and feelings, as something separated from the rest – a kind of optical delusion of his consciousness. This delusion is a kind of prison for us, restricting us to our personal desires and......to affection for a few persons nearest us. Our task must be to free ourselves from the prison by widening our circles of compassion to embrace all living creatures and the whole of nature in its beauty.

- Albert Einstein

When looking through spiritual eyes, one of the most quoted phrases in the bible could read: For God (Wholeness) so loved the world (objective experience) he gave his only begotten son (subjective experience) that whoever believeth in him (faith) shall have everlasting life (infinity). Gives it a whole new perspective.

My aim for this book is to convey a model which best describes the nature of *your* reality. What has struck me on my search is how everything appears paradoxical. At the superficial day-to-day level of our existence we are, for the most part, unaware of how life functions as a paradox. It must. This is to allow the story to be told from different points of view and as I'm sure you well know - everyone has a point of view!

The mistake we commonly make is to attribute labels of right and wrong as if they are facts. What might appear as a fact to you might not be the case for another. A lot of people find this very difficult to accept.

"Think for yourselves and let others enjoy the privilege to do so, too."

-Voltaire

Science has fallen into the trap of trying to create a model for ultimate reality, this I believe is infinite....... therefore unknowable. Science at its core is rooted in mathematics – the art of measurement. Mathematics at its core is rooted in the empty set – which is nothing, therefore unmeasurable. Both nothing and infinity are one and the same with both being unmeasurable therefore fundamental and unknowable at least from humanities standpoint. We must acknowledge that science and mathematics are a tool of consciousness not the other way around. It is possible to become aware of the fundamental principles at play, but the obsession to know quite often clouds that which we are eternally aware of. A balance between thoughts and feelings is required to walk the middle path.

"Middle path is the balanced path –
seeing the 'complete truth' instead of
illusionary 'half truth'."

-Buddha

The complete truth is not fixed: nothing is. The complete truth needs to be flexible and malleable to accommodate change for the purpose of evolution. Do not mistake evolution for Darwinian evolution. Darwinian evolution is just a story arising from the connection of biological systems. If all things come from the one source then connections would be expected. It has always been incomplete as it breaks down at the fundamental level. It is based on the common assumption that a solid material world exists outside of any conscious entity being present. I aim to show this is not the case and put forth a fundamental system which is all inclusive at every scale. The evolution I am referring to is the patterns of growth which lead to greater self-awareness. It's opposite, involution, is built into the system from the points of view.......Us. I believe evolution comes from a perfect inner spiral linked to the golden mean ratio which manifests outwardly as the imperfect Fibonacci sequence to bring about variation. Mathematicians have known about the golden mean spiral way back (I use the term loosely) to the ancient Greeks and I'm sure beyond, but more recently have struggled with why this is. It can all be linked to fractal geometrical systems none of which are taught in schools. An understanding of this can lead to empowerment of the individual by helping people think for themselves. We live in a system that is quite the opposite. The question you need to ask yourself is - is it time for change?

Mathematics, symbols and linguistics codify our stories about existence and provide clues to our true nature and the principles of reality. Mathematics enlightens through shapes, sets and patterns. Symbols are representative of an object, function or process, and linguistics provides us with the ability for communication through meaning and inference. Also if you look closely enough at the structure of particular words you can find a hidden meaning. This being the case then ask yourself who would put it there and why?

Like a true detective you can piece together the clues contained within mathematics, symbols and linguistics and observe the patterns and principles that life or consciousness presents before you. When you realise and accept this as true you can really appreciate and embrace the magnificent wonder of life.

My advice: Never let anyone convince you that you are an accident of chance, that by happenstance you become consciously self-aware and are insignificant within the vastness of the entire universe. You most certainly are not! Read on and let's see if I can convince you of your true identity.

CHAPTER 1

Life is Paradoxical

"It is paradoxical, yet true, to say that the more we know, the more ignorant we become in the absolute sense, for it is only through enlightenment that we become conscious of our limitations. Precisely one of the most gratifying results of intellectual evolution is the continuous opening up of new and greater prospects."

-Nikola Tesla

So what is a paradox? A paradox is a statement or proposition that despite sound reasoning from acceptable premises leads to a conclusion that seems senseless, logically unacceptable or self-contradictory. Take a moment and contemplate on the statement "I am a liar".

1

We live in a world of paradoxes, we just don't realise it. Paradoxes exist everywhere. One of the most recognisable is the chicken and egg paradox. Which came first, the chicken or the egg? This is a fundamental clue to life, what life really is and how it has come into being.

The current scientific thinking is that chemicals arranged themselves randomly in such a way that a primordial bacteria developed to evolve, think and go on to develop self-awareness: Really? This provides no explanation for the chicken and egg paradox.

How is it possible for something as inanimate as matter to become sentient? As it stands, science has no creditable answer. At the outset of my spiritual journey I also discovered much to my surprise that science for all its wonderful contributions in technology and other major advances cannot define fundamentally what time is. Add to that mass, length, gravity, light, electricity, magnetism and numbers - what everything is built upon. The list goes on and on. We are aware of them on a daily basis and take their presence for granted. For the world to exist and everything to coexist this is the way it has to be. The paradoxical nature is built into the system and for the most part we are blinded to this. When I first realised this it acted as a catalyst which fuelled my desire to know more.

A lot of what I was conditioned to believe to be true has turned out to be built on foundations of quicksand, sinking slowly into the depths of nothingness. Paradoxically when I reached this nothing it turned into something, but not only something, it turned into everything dependent on how I looked at it. The deeper I dug the more profound life became. The more self-aware I became. Out of a sense of complete isolation and at times desolation I began to grow and reconnect. I began to realise that all is not lost - in fact the complete opposite is true. Nothing can ever be lost as it really has nowhere to go in the first place. What we perceive as 'nowhere' is really 'now here'. It is all based on how we look at it, the perspective we take. It is all based around which story we tell ourselves about what it is we are looking for and our beliefs related to this story.

3

How ironic would it be to discover that most of what you were told as you were growing up is the opposite of what life actually appears to be? Most of us were conditioned to believe we are victims of circumstance, that we react to situations as opposed to creating them and that a higher power is continually judging and assessing whether we're fit to progress to the next level or forever burn in the pits of hell. We are told God is love, but if you piss him off he develops amnesia. He also seems for some reason to need a lot of money. I make no excuse in this age of overzealous political correctness when referencing God as male as that is how I was conditioned in the environment I grew up in. How easy it is to condition someone!

Mum "ok kids it's Sunday, time to go to church."

Kids "Do we really have to? We want to stay home and play and have fun."

Mum "Don't be silly, Sunday's a day of rest. You're not allowed to have fun!"

When left unchallenged the kids grow up to become parents themselves and subject their children to the same conditioned diatribe they were subjected to. This conditioning is related to nurture and the debate still rages about which it is, nature or nurture? Paradoxically both are depending on one's point of view at any given moment, but it could be claimed that nurture is a natural process and therefore must be enfolded within nature. You could say nurture is life's expression and nature is the birthing seed.

Let's take a deeper look at some of the more challenging paradoxes that exist and you will come to see how they are all interconnected.

The Spiritual Paradox

Let's begin at the beginning......or the end.......or maybe somewhere in between. You see fundamentally there is no beginning and there is no end. Fundamentally there just is. At the source of all, there is total stillness, a well of nothingness or, to borrow a quote from the Buddha, "a void of infinite potential".

Let's take a deeper look. A void can be defined as "completely empty". Infinite is limitless, unbounded, and potential is defined in the Oxford English Dictionary as "having the capacity to become or develop into something in the future". Personally I think a better description would be "being the capacity to become something in the future". When referencing future we are always talking from our perspective. Past and future only come about in the reality we create from our point of view. Ultimate reality has no past or future; 'all that is' just is. Being is born in the present, resides in the present and dies in the present. In effect being never leaves the present, it is present moment awareness.

To be, or not to be, that is the question

-Shakespeare

So....the void of infinite potential can be thought of as "a completely empty unbounded nothingness in an eternal moment with the capacity to become all things in time". Here I feel we have a wonderful description of Spirit. We could use the terms consciousness, awareness, source or higher self in place of Spirit, but for the most part I will stick with Spirit, although all four terms are relevant.

The world's foremost religions attribute Spirit with the characteristics of omnipotence, omniscience and omnipresence. All powerful, all knowing and everywhere. Christianity quite often uses the term Holy Ghost in place of Spirit. By a simple spelling tweak we can replace the word Holy with Wholly and Ghost with Spirit and we end up with Spirit as the whole shooting match, being "all that is" physically and metaphysically; the seen and the unseen.

The human mind likes to construct order out of chaos. To do so it requires tools. For the purpose of definition the mind requires the ability to create the illusion of separateness by boxing things to perceive them as objects. For this to happen, the mind needs to construct the ultimate box or container for everything to take place within. This container is space and time. Of course the terminology used is metaphorical with no physical container actually existing. No physical anything actually exists but paradoxically you can, through your choosing, experience as if it does. For every increment you perceive as a second, you create 186 200 miles when your focus of attention is maximised i.e. when looking at a star. This is known as the speed of light or the universal constant. This would be better described as the speed of causality. The speed at which you correlate with something else within your frame of reference, in other words your reality tunnel. This something else is energy. We are unable to define what energy is, we only have the ability to interpret what it does or the influence it has on an event. Mentally, from your perspective, with you being the deciding factor to any circumstance and with everyone else having the same privilege, we now encounter the mental paradox. The paradox of the one and the many.

Order and chaos are inextricably linked. Chaos must also exist for order to exist. If we think of order as the seen, the physical world, then the unseen can be thought of as chaos, the metaphysical reality. Enter quantum theory. This is the science of the micro world, the building blocks of nature. Except there are no blocks, no any-'thing' for that matter. Quantum theory is really, I believe, the science of spirit. From the human perspective the quantum world is counter intuitive. It does not correspond to logic and reason. This being the case it can be viewed as totally chaotic. At the quantum level every-'thing' is considered to exist in a state of superposition. From the perspective of viewing it from this level an ordered state re-emerges. Superposition is a state in which everything exists as waves of potential in a field system all at the same time. A field in physics terms is a physical quantity associated with every point of spacetime. Please note the use of the word physical is referring to the manifestation of energy at every point of spacetime which is in effect non-physical (a paradox). This field has no boundaries therefore everything exists everywhere and nowhere at the same time. Within superposition is every possible outcome. Can you see the likeness to spirit? The image manifests as a probability wave of what is the next most likely outcome of a mental event, created by an observer from the field of all possibilities.

The spiritual paradox manifests through you as the creator of your reality tunnel along with everyone else creating their reality tunnels collectively, known as ultimate reality, as seen from your point of view. The key here is 'from your point of view' as all paradoxes are created mentally not spiritually. Paradoxically there is no spiritual paradox. Once again it is the paradox of the one and the many.

The Mental Paradox of Time

Let's now consider the paradox of time. Time requires a beginning and an end. Eternity does not. The human mind struggles to comprehend eternity just like infinity. Why?...because it's the human mind where time is created in the first place. Time is a mental construct created by you. It is subjective. It is also paradoxical. As we have established your spiritual essence is timeless, but the human you, also referred to as your ego, is time based.

In everyday life you wake up, look at the clock and visualise where you have to be when. You have formed a relationship with all clocks, watches and the numerous time pieces that have been constructed throughout the ages. But what really is this method of keeping time? What is it based upon?

This method of keeping time is based upon the perception of movement. As you appear to walk along the street the concept of time passes in a linear fashion; one moment after the next. When you are sitting in the living room of your house watching television time passes in a linear fashion. Even when you are lying down in your bed time still appears to pass linearly. In each case movement is occurring all of the time or at least the perception of movement is occurring constantly. No matter whether you are standing, sitting or sleeping the Earth continues to spin and travel through space. Therefore you are never in the same place.....ever! You are always on the move. Things are always changing.

Change is the only constant.

-Heraclitus

Another way to consider this is through the co-ordinates of Space and Time or what Einstein referred to as "Spacetime". This is also referred to as the Spacetime continuum. In the free dictionary this is defined as: the four dimensional continuum, having three spacial co-ordinates and one temporal co-ordinate, in which all physical qualities may be located. Note the word temporal in place of time. This as I mentioned earlier is not a physical quality it is a mental one. Main stream science makes the assumption that at the fundamental level of existence the world is material i.e. made from solid particles, so the fact that it also incorporates Einstein's Spacetime continuum within its doctrine then throws up another paradox; The paradox of material and immaterial.

In our everyday reality we measure time in increments - seconds being the base rate. But pause for a second or two and think "what really is a second?"...... A second is related to the movement of the Earth's rotation and its orbit around the Sun. One full cycle we call a year. We break this down into months, weeks, days, hours, minutes and seconds. Note how it's a twofold process. Time is related to not only the earth's axial rotation (which gives us a day) but also the earth's orbit of the Sun (which gives us a year). Life tends to utilise two things to create variation. This is very important. Lookout for the twofold patterns, they are everywhere. Why?...... Because Spirit in human form experiences itself in the realm of duality. When this is understood the mystery of life begins to unveil itself.

This dual nature of time has been best described by Einstein in his revelation of Special Relativity. Special

Relativity provides us with the realisation that time is observer dependent. You being the observer. If time is temporal then it must be you as the observer who is creating subjectively the mental perception of time. We all know from our own experiences that time varies depending on how excited or bored we are.

Husband "How was your day dear?"

Wife "I sat in the office for hours with little to do, it seemed like an eternity. What about you?"

Husband "Mine flew...... I met somebody I hadn't seen in years and we had so much to catch up on."

Wife "You must get yourself a job!"

Einstein's 1905 paper on Special Relativity turned the concept of time on its head. The mechanical nature of time previously held as true was banished to the annals of, well......time.

It took many years before Special Relativity was accepted by the scientific community as the way things appear to be. The speed of clocks vary depending on where the observer is in relation to what is being measured and the velocities of both the observer and the observed. This was a seismic shift in thinking. But today most people still function in a clockwork society giving Einstein's approach no real credence. We are so consumed with ourselves in our day-to-day existence that the bigger picture for the most part doesn't appear to really matter. What we don't realise is that by doing so, we ultimately enslave ourselves as victims of time.

The Paradox of Now

What is 'now'? Is it the present time? Well……..no it can't be. You see time as we have said is measured in increments, but to attempt to measure 'now' is impossible because measurement is a process that requires time and in that time required, to measure now, has vanished. Yet……it is always now. It can never not be now. Therefore we must conclude 'now' is eternal. The question then arises, if 'now' is eternal and every experience you ever had only happens in the eternal moment of 'now', does that make you eternal?

The Mental Paradox of Space

"Space: the final frontier. These are the voyages of the Starship Enterprise. It's five-year mission; to explore strange new worlds, to seek out new life and new civilisations, to boldly go where no man has gone before".

Most of us will recognise this statement narrated by William Shatner at the beginning of all but one of the original Star Trek episodes. The space in question would be better termed "outer space" as space is also what differentiates all objects here on earth too. Our sensory organs interpret space as empty. But here's the kicker, the space that we perceive which is pretty much everywhere is infinitely dense. Calculations show the energy in one cubic centimetre of volume of space is 10^{93} grams. That is a 10 followed by 93 zeros, but we really don't have much to compare this against, even when we consider all the mass in the universe has been calculated to be 10^{55} grams. So you can see what we will term the vacuum density is not empty space at all, but is close to forty orders of magnitude greater. It is an ocean of motion brimming full of energy and information.

So how can your body move through something which is infinitely dense? There are two ways to interpret this. The first is that your body just happens to be made of the same infinitely dense atoms as the vacuum therefore no energy differential exists between the two except that which is caused by inertia: Newton's first law of motion. The second is even more profound. The universe you perceive is a holographic illusion you create as a playground to experience the story you are telling yourself. This in essence is a non-solid mental world within which your senses perceive signals vibrating at various frequencies which creates a reality that appears solid and 'out there' but ironically is not. Paradoxically something infinitely dense can also appear as totally transparent, it all depends on where you are looking from. Therefore what we think of as space is all enfolded within a dynamically perpetual information exchanging system which we have previously referred to as Spirit. This helps to enlighten us to the belief systems which perpetuate an omnipotent, omnipresent and omniscient being.

The Paradox of Self

Relativity arises from the word relationship. Essentially it is your relationship with something else that you perceive not to be you within a frame of reference. The frame of reference arises because our mental perceptions require separation for a benchmark to relate to, for meaning to be added. We also put a mental box around things to define what they are. Then in our human guise we have an experience. The world that we have the experience in is of dual nature. This duality is constructed by the mind. Although duality appears as a two-fold process it is in reality three-fold. The three things are; you the subject, the object you are relating to and the frame of reference it is experienced within, or simply put; subject, object and the space in between.

This is because we are multidimensional beings. We operate on three main levels: Mind, Body and Spirit. Certain religions call it Father, Son and the Holy Ghost. Science refers to it as the Mental, Physical and Metaphysical realms although it tends to shy away from anything metaphysical as the scientific method struggles to substantiate proof in this area. The metaphysical realm tends to operate subjectively from points of view. This is all related to probable outcomes, the probability bell curve which arises and the statistical analysis it produces. Think of the metaphysical as possibility and the physical as probability.

There is a link between probable outcomes and peoples points of view. Probably much greater than what is realised, excuse the pun. Everyone has a point of view, whether they choose to share it is up to them, it is their divine right! You are born a free spirit but usually end up shackled by society's rules, regulations, laws and morality. Society tends to distort and influence how you think and react. Paradoxically this is by divine intention. Your ego is defined by habitual nature. It is the label that follows the "I am" that you believe yourself to be, but are not. Some wise ass a long time ago was asked "who are you?" he replied "I am that I am".........he hit the nail on the head. Fundamentally you are not the labels you use to define yourself; your ego. You are not the six foot two Hollywood movie star with the chiselled good looks. You are not the grey haired retired charity shop assistant with a touch of arthritis. You are not the spotty insecure teenager who mopes about thinking the worlds against them. Your ego may try to blind you to this, but you are not any of these and yet paradoxically you are all of the above! Fundamentally you are the free spirit you always have been and always will be. The spirit which tells every story. The choices you make and the story you tell yourself, from the moment you awaken to the moment you go to sleep and even the dreams you concoct, is the human you. The 'self' comes in different guises with yourself and every other individual self-enfolded within the 'one spiritual' self. The paradox of how the one is the many and the many are the one or as Rumi put it "You are not a drop in the ocean. You are the entire ocean in a drop".

The human paradox

Ask anybody the question "Who are you?" And for the most part they will tell you their name. You are not your name. Your name is a label your parents gave you when you were born. If you dig a little deeper generally you will hear (accompanied by a slightly quizzical look) "I am my body". Again you are not your body. Your body is a vessel you perceive the world through with your nervous system. Your nervous system does this by receiving and decoding signals oscillating at differing vibrational frequencies. When you reduce your body to its base building blocks you discover there is nothing there. Nature's atomic structure from which everything is made, including your body, is all part of the electromagnetic spectrum through which the universe springs forth. The visible spectrum we observe, which is all of the light in the universe only accounts for approximately three percent of the total spectrum which gives you an idea of the size. Interestingly the Standard model of the universe in cosmology can only account for approximately three percent of its mass......I wonder? Anyway your body does not define the real you. The next answer might be "I am my thoughts", but the question arises, who then is the observer behind your thoughts? Contemplate for a moment on the awareness of being able to think......by not thinking. Deep meditation goes to a place of no thought. Just observing with no labels or judgements achieves the same state. When you achieve this state you become aware that you are aware.

In many traditions this observer is known as the silent witness. The presence that is always present. Call it what you like. It is that which abides within that just is. Spirit or God are the common labels, but do not mistake this presence for the anthropometric God of religion. God is not made in the image and likeness of man in a way a lot of religions depict. As kids we grow up being told stories of God up in the clouds or heavens with a bushy beard looking down on us and judging if we have played the game of life within his rules. As children we absorb information like sponges which form sub-conscious programmes which we can carry for the rest of our lives if we don't question them. This programming is evident in every aspect of our lives, so my advice is to tread carefully with what we fill the younger generations heads with. This, I hope you would agree, is not what God is like. The interpretation that God is made in the image and likeness of man as we perceive our human selves is misleading. In any case the biblical statement reads "Man is made in the image and likeness of God". God is generally not the best term to use. We have too many of our own preconditions attached to our personal conception of who and what God is like, stemming mostly from our childhood. A more appropriate description I believe is Spirit.

Let's revisit the previous statement replacing the word God with Spirit. Spirit is not made in the image and likeness of Man. Man is made in the image and likeness of Spirit. With Spirit being "the void of infinite potential" then, if we also replace image with imagination, what we have is "Man is made in the imagination with the infinite potential of Spirit." It would appear its man's own imagination which is the real creative power in the universe. Can you now begin to appreciate, even a little bit, your true identity?

Man is nothing (no-thing in particular) so then paradoxically Man must be everything. What if Man is short for Manifestation? Manifestation is defined as an object that clearly shows or embodies something abstract or theoretical. Let's substitute YOU for the object that is embodied and, with abstract defined as 'existing in thought or as an idea but not having a physical or concrete existence', let's substitute YOUR reality tunnel (the world you perceive 'out there'). Manifestation, YOU, are bringing into action through imagination something abstract, the world YOU perceive, using the infinite potential power of your higher self which is Spirit. This is very important to try to come to terms with. When you can wrap your head around this you can begin to realise your connection with your spiritual self and the power you have to co-create all of your dreams.

> "All matter is merely energy condensed to a slow vibration that we are all one consciousness experiencing itself subjectively, there is no such thing as death, life is only a dream, and we are the imagination of ourselves."

> -Bill Hicks

Neville Goddard an amazing 20th century spiritual orator believed God to be the human imagination. Listening to what he had to say and how he said it, you might find it hard to disagree with him. He was extremely eloquent in his portrayal of who we are and our relationship with God (Spirit).

So what exactly is our imagination? It would appear according to Neville it has a lot to live up to. The suffix "ation" means "action" so imagination would be image-in-action. If you think of image as a mental picture this would suggest it is an internal image which is actioned outwardly. In physics terms action is angular momentum. We know momentum is motion of a moving body, so action is movement or what we perceive as movement due to it arising from a series of snapshots translated by your brain. This is also translated as the passage of time. So why angular? This is related to spin and produces a spiral based on the phi ratio which is the driving force behind change. In psychology tests have shown that even when we recall a vivid memory it is never exactly the same.

The true sign of intelligence is not knowledge, but imagination

-Albert Einstein

The paradox of being human or as we usually term it, a human being, is the illusion or probably better put, the delusion, of our false belief about ourselves. We mistake the mental experience we have of ourselves with an actual thing in and of itself. You see yourself as separate in some ways isolated and alone. Nothing could be further from the truth. Everything is connected.

As a Human Being the basis for your life is to experience. Everything you do, become or are aware of is meaningful experience.

For you to have any meaningful experience you require a benchmark. For the mind (which is not the brain) to decide what anything means, it must have something to relate it to. In quantum physics this is known as subject-object relationship. You are the subjective observer forever putting meaning to objective reality.

This correlation I believe is done at light speed by your subconscious but your conscious focus can only perform one thing at a time - although very quickly. Your conscious focus darts all over the place but is limited to snapshots. These snapshots in which your 'out there' experiences take place within is what Einstein labelled "Spacetime". Spacetime is a set of co-ordinates, three spacial dimensions and one time, in which you construct a mental picture that is put together within your mind but in a delusional sense we perceive it all to exist outside of ourselves.

More and more people are awakening to this. The belief that objective reality is really a perceptual delusion on your part. That there is no "out there" only an "in here".

> "All that we see and seem is but a dream within a dream"
>
> -Edgar Allan Poe

Let's take a look linguistically at the label Human Being. We know that Being just is. It is an absolute term and linking you to your spiritual self. Being is always timeless. If man is manifestation then what does the pre-fix Hu mean? The pre-fix Hu is the name of God in Sufism. It is literally Arabic for the English 'He'. It is "God, just he", or "God himself". Let's put it altogether. A human being is "God himself manifesting eternally through the expression of you". Could this be the greatest paradox of all?

Of course, this is my story being told from my point of view. None of what I put forth should be accepted at face value. We all have the divine right to contemplate and question everything and should never give that power away.

A friend once told me with extreme certainty, "nobody can know how it all began and what it's all about!". This I believe is what we commonly refer to as an oxymoron.

At the level of mind, body and spirit it would appear the mind's contribution of linking spirit to the bodily experience is the creator of the paradox. So how and why does it function in this way?

CHAPTER 2

Feedback Loops

Opposites are complementary. At first this statement might appear nonsense, but with closer inspection we realise you can't have one without the other. Everything has its opposite whether it's obvious or not. It's the only way the mind can put meaning to anything. Each individual mind correlates the extremes based upon its current knowledge base on the subject matter and comes to a decision which usually lies somewhere between the two. As you can imagine everyone differs in their knowledge base and their interpretation. This allows for infinite variety of decisions and choice.

The epistemological process

One of the main branches of philosophy is epistemology. The theory of knowledge. How do we know what we know? That I cannot answer directly, but I am convinced the process used is the mental law of opposite's feedback loop which is based on the power of three. In this case the power of three is otherwise known as the wholly trinity – the ultimate ménage à trois. In Manchester they think it's Best, Law and Charlton, but I beg to differ! The wholly trinity is really the origin of infinity from a set of three from the perspective of the mind. This is so important! The realisation of perspective even at the fundamental level. Whose eyes are you looking through? From the spiritual perspective one, two and three are meaningless. It's you as self-awareness that is putting the meaning to everything - material and abstract. I see the mind as the process within this set of three connecting you at the self-aware level to the higher self, that of absolute awareness or consciousness. The mind also functions as a three-fold process: knowing, choosing and interpreting. This is the process connecting absolute awareness (spirit) to self-awareness (you). Likewise there is no first or second, one did not come before the other. Existence requires all three conditions to be wrapped up altogether at the same time in one eternal moment. This is where the English language can let us down somewhat. We conceptualise linked to the language used when talking to ourselves. I am led to believe the language of the Hopi Indian which has no past or future tense can explain Einstein's relativity much more eloquently than English. Can't see it being much good for composing a script for a Hollywood movie though. Unfortunately for us they neglected to teach

Hopi at my school and if I was a betting man I would guess yours too - so English it is. Anyhow, absolute awareness is all knowing......you, on the other hand, are a self-aware activity through knowledge and what you decide it means to you for the purpose of having an experience, as does everyone else, which makes up the totality of absolute awareness. Awareness and all the activities of self-awareness are connected through a feedback loop system of information exchange. Each informs the other for the purpose of evolution.

It's all a matter of feedback

One of the best representations of a feedback loop process is the infinity symbol. Think of it in three dimensions rather than two; where the crossover point doesn't actually come into contact. You can imagine how perpetual motion can take place around the infinity symbol when there is no loss of energy.

When information is exchanged in the outer world, energy is required. This system of energy conversion and loss leads eventually to death. This for us takes place at the cellular level. The bodies we mentally construct are composed of a community of up to 100 trillion cells for the most part living in harmony, keeping our hearts beating, lungs pumping, brains functioning etc...... This all happens subconsciously allowing you to focus your attention on things that elicit feelings of joy or sorrow......it's up to you! At times and in specific areas of the body dis-ease occurs when the information exchange at the cellular level breaks down. According to the wonderful research conducted by Professor Bruce Lipton the brain of the cell is not in the nucleus, it is the cells outer skin. This ironically is called the membrane. The membrane is the cells interface with the outside environment. The cell in essence is a product of its environment with the membrane acting as a transmitter/receiver of information in the form of signals of varying frequency incorporating feedback. This is also an apt description of the human brain which is always in contact with the cells. What we have is a fractal system of a similar repeating pattern at different scales. It is also a great example of how feedback not only exists at the spiritual (awareness/self-awareness) level, but also at the spiritual/biological level. The nature of growth requires feedback whether that be spiritual, mental or biological.

The exchange of information at the universal level, in which your body participates, requires energy, and the second law of thermodynamics dictates heat cannot of itself get hotter. We can therefore conclude, without feedback or efficient feedback, that a system - whether that be biological or mechanical - will eventually cease. This I will stress again is at the level of experience, the world we perceive out there. We tell ourselves there are only two sure things in life – death and taxes. Well maybe not the case. Apparently if you are head of the International Monetary Fund, which basically exists because of taxation, you are not required to pay tax. With this irony in mind maybe death is an illusion also. So what I am saying is a feedback loop can stop functioning if it is not being constantly topped up.

Can perpetual motion exist? Is it possible for a system to continue to function at its maximum without loss of energy? At the spiritual level this would appear to be the case. At this level time does not exist. Due to this, no sequence of events is required therefore no energy loss. All opposites are entangled and really exist as one in a state of potential. It's the perspective of the mind from a point of view which creates the differential and the illusion of separation. Hence the arrival of time. The creation of time comes about when we combine our experiences into a story format. At the same time another joins the party. Hi! Let me introduce myself......they call me Memory, and if you can remember......so can you.

At the spiritual or absolute level of all possible persons, places, circumstances and events (possibilities) time has no relevance. This is a non-local realm where there are no co-ordinates for the purpose of localising an object at a point in space at a particular time. Paradoxically everything exists everywhere and nowhere all in the same moment. We all have the mental ability to dip into this realm for the purpose of extracting information into a format to have an experience and then feed it back immediately. By doing so there is no measurable loss of energy and yet, paradoxically, a copy has been made which decays immediately (the unmeasurable moment of now), but leaves traces of information/energy behind that we call memories. The paradox unveils itself when we contemplate on the moment of now and how it can never be captured - or can it? Is a photograph or video footage (which is a series of still frames, one after the other processed by the brain at a particular speed for the perception of movement) the now moment imprisoned? Once again it comes down to the perspective it's viewed from. On one side the answer would appear to be a resounding 'yes!' A photograph is information within a frame of reference captured at a particular moment. Only one moment can truly exist so the elusive now has been tamed. Or......you can see it the opposite way, that it can't be now in the photograph because I'm looking at it......now. This could spaghettify your mind!!! Let's be honest, if life unveiled itself in a straightforward easily understood manner there would be no mystery. No mystery......no evolution.

A conscious observer must always be present in 'all ways' for the system to flourish. The mental feedback loop is metaphorical yet always is. It will never cease. For this reason death is not an option for the consciousness you exhibit. For the purpose of understanding we could say you are hard wired into the system. You can only observe and perceive the death of objective reality 'from your point of view' from this level of conscious awareness which also includes your body. Conscious awareness never dies as there is nothing else for it to become and nowhere for it to go. It is eternally non-local! Contemplation of non-existence is impossible. There is no 'the end' of your consciousness because there was never a beginning. We are so conditioned to think 'in time' that eternity and infinity are alien concepts. This is the paradox of you. The outer you and the inner you are opposites. One being time constrained and finite, the other eternal and infinite. Yet the law of opposites tells us both are one and the same. When you programme your mind to become aware of this you will see the same self-similar patterns everywhere.

It's all entangled

This fundamental law of opposites feedback loop system based on the power of three things can also be thought of as a tangled hierarchy in which two things require each other with the third being the process or connector of the two. Another example is memory requires perception, but to have a perception you require memory. Contemplate for a moment on this......if all of your memories where completely erased how would you know anything? Would it not be the case that from your point of view it would feel like your initial moment of birth? No history, no beliefs, no language skills etc......With this in mind it would suggest the moment a memory is stored, or to put it better, the ability for recollection is your birth 'in time'. The answer always lies from the perspective taken. At the cellular level when the membrane of the initial cell requires a memory for interaction with its environment (the spark of self-awareness) this could suggest cellular birth into time based reality.

Another perspective is when the same function takes place, but at the embryonic brain stage. Could this be considered the moment of birth? This all takes place within the womb from which the perspective of the cell and the embryo see as the outer world. From the perspective of the parents this all takes place in the inner world and the baby doesn't enter their outer world until its journey through, for the most part, the birth canal. As you can see perspective is fundamental to the 'Whole' system but at the biological level this tends to lead to confusion and disagreements in the world in which we co-exist.

It's the chicken…..no it's the egg…..well actually

What we can draw from all of this is how the feedback loop and perspective are connected. A perspective can be taken from any point along the feedback loop. Let's revisit the chicken and egg paradox armed with this knowledge. We know the answer is based on the perspective taken and due to this being a fundamental question, the possibilities are more restricted. The potential answers are:-

1) The chicken
2) The egg
3) Both
4) Neither

This is known as a quantum event. On the other hand a classical computer operates using bits comprised of 1's and 0's, similar to an on/off switch. It is either one or the other. For the left hemisphere of the brain this makes perfect sense. This is where logic resides. Walk into a darkened room flick the switch the bulb lights up......hey presto! Flick the switch the opposite way the light goes off. All well and good. At this point the left hemisphere is wondering what's the purpose of my next door neighbour......the right? I've got this all under control.....thinks logic! Things start to go slightly awry when on another occasion I saunter into the room and with a logical swagger flick the switch and nothing happens. "Hang about what's going on here?" flashes by. "Where did that come from?" "It's me your other half, I'm the right hemisphere and I'm here for creativity amongst other things. Could it be a power cut, maybe a short circuit or is a blown fuse the problem? Has the switch depressed fully, or could the bulb be the issue" is my right hemisphere's creative response. Suddenly a scenario arises that logic has difficulty dealing with. The point being, although the world appears on the surface as dual nature it is all built upon quantum events. Quantum events are not logical! Quantum events allow you to create the story of your choosing through your belief system. Take note of this – it's you who decides what you believe to be true. You may be influenced by others, but the final decision always rests with you.

In comparison a quantum computer's output ranges from 1 to zero and every possibility in between. This is known as a qubit. A qubit then is subject to every possible outcome, so what or who influences the outcome? When a quantum computation takes place the answer always involves the bias of who is asking (usually referenced as the observer). This sounds totally counter intuitive and the reason so many scientists and people in general struggle with the quantum world. The bias comes from previously downloaded programmes the observer has accepted as their truth or belief system. The most famous of all quantum experiments, the double slit, has been performed in a multitude of ways for a century now, always leading to the same conclusion......you as the observer decide the outcome wittingly or unwittingly. How often does this take place? Would it surprise you to know it happens every moment you are consciously aware? From the perspective of thought you process information at the quantum level with your very own personal quantum processor......your brain. It has been suggested there are as many neuronal network combinations in your brain as there are atoms in the known universe. How amazing is that? Your brain correlates so much information at the same time it is quite staggering!

"It from Bit symbolises the idea that every item of the physical world has at bottom an immaterial source and

explanation.......that all things physical
are information-theoretic in origin and
that this is a participatory universe."

-John Archibald Wheeler

Your brain is an organ that appears physical in
nature. It is connected through the 'body interface'
with the environment, which receives and transmits
information by, and as, the quantum field. It does this
by decoding, converting and projecting mental signals
broadcast by the mind. The purpose of the brain is not
for thinking. No brain has ever had a thought in its life.
The neuronal network is the hardware and operational
software that converts electrical stimuli into chemical
responses and 'actioned' events programmed by
the mind. (The now moment only really exists from
the perspective of observation 'without thought' in
the spiritual realm. When the boundary condition
is crossed into our world of events, with thought
being a process requiring time, the moment of now
translates as a memory therefore is an actioned
event as opposed to an action event. I believe what
we perceive as the moment of now from our point
of view is really a memory). This is carried out by
the unlimited potential of spirit being the conscious
operator inputting the next choice and receiving the
feedback of the experience. The mind acts like the
software programmes that run the show, but always

requires a conscious programmer to write them in the first place.

> "My brain is only a receiver, in the universe there is a core from which we obtain knowledge, strength and inspiration. I have not penetrated into the secrets of this core, but I know that it exists."
>
> -Nikola Tesla

The real ultimate question

At the level of ultimate reality, the spiritual level of pure conscious awareness, the chicken and egg question is totally irrelevant as time does not exist. First and second only matter in our time-based construct of reality which is always 'souly' from our point of view or perspective. Paradoxes like this are clues to a more fundamental reality than the mind. To attempt to answer the question is 'mental' torture, but does give us a glimpse of our true infinite nature. The key is...... you are aware the paradox exists. This awareness is consciousness.

A paradox is information in which two extremes require each other and are entangled in a feedback loop and cannot be resolved at the level of the mind. The mind is the process in which information flows. Mentally a paradox is information flowing perpetually. This is the minds connection to infinity. It demonstrates the futile attempt to 'know' what consciousness or ultimate reality really is. Demonstrate being the key word. We all have the ability to demonstrate consciousness which we do every day. So demonstrate your highest version of self as often as you can to 'realise' your true self.

The current mainstream model based on mathematical and scientific principles hates infinities. Scientists go to extraordinary lengths to remove infinity from their equations. Why? If we conclude everything to be infinite, at the source, then intelligent design is irrefutable and that being the case it leads to a dissatisfied ego. The ego is finite, bounded and craves to be in control. The ego likes things to be defined and in their place because this type of feedback strengthens the ego's belief in itself. It provides a false sense of self which mirrors the true self that hides behind the veil allowing the ego to flourish. What we have on one side of the boundary is the one true self existing in an eternal, infinite and unbounded state, having need for nothing and being nothing (no-thing in particular). On the other side we have the ego believing itself to be something, wanting to do anything and feeling the need to have everything. We are always see-sawing between the two. The ego resides in the material world and through the beliefs it accumulates over time creates separation. It is finite, bounded and operates in a time-based reality or so it thinks yet paradoxically the ego also exists as infinity because in each moment change has occurred and it recreates itself anew. The ego itself is also split and can be witnessed and experienced superficially in the extreme as split personality disorder. It functions in a dual natured reality which deepens the mystery even more. Do you see the pattern? This is the universal law of opposites at play which is held together by a network of feedback loops constructed mentally. As you can see it's this network of mental feedback loops that are at the root of the paradoxes.

I'll scratch your back – you scratch mine

Feedback is the principle that binds the whole show. Without feedback the universe would exist in total chaos with nothing relating to anything else. Every moment of your existence involves feedback and with this being the case you would expect some sort of underlying intelligence orchestrating the 'whole' affair. A Rubix cube has been calculated to have 43 quintillion permutations. If a blind man with no visual or verbal feedback of information makes a move every second, it has been calculated it would take longer than the 13.8 billion years the universe is believed to have existed to complete the cube. With feedback all cubes can be completed within 20 moves when the required knowledge has been amassed. What a difference! Even the current scientific paradigms belief in an infinity of parallel universes, the multiverse, with this one being the goldilocks version, still crumbles when you acknowledge the extent feedback is required on a moment to moment basis. The multiverse being somewhat of an oxymoron considering the current paradigm's ignorance of infinity!

If we accept everything is connected and everything is fundamentally one, it would follow the same principles should apply for feedback loops. It would suggest feedback loops are embedded within feedback loops all stemming from a source feedback loop. The most fundamental feedback loop I believe to be the one and the many. The feedback loop that one is the many (infinity) and the many are the one. This is at the source of spiritual wholeness. The whole thing (infinity) divides itself into an infinity of activities with each activity containing all of the information of the whole thing, with each perpetually feeding back its personal experience of the information. This is the ultimate one and the many feedback loop. There are many other feedback loops embedded within this. Let's take a look at some more.

My heads in a spin

It is said the singularity is complete stillness. Both the scientific and spiritual perspectives appear to agree on this. Science has confirmed that everything contains spin whether we realise it or not. From a well of absolute stillness chaos springs forth with incredible velocity, spinning at unbelievable speeds. At one point we have total stillness, no movement whatsoever, just pure potential. As we add a spinning vibratory force we perceive movement in the form of oscillation. As the speed increases it gets to a point when the spin is so fast that it appears still once more. You could say stillness is the accumulation of all spin. Stillness and movement are inextricably linked through angular momentum. Interestingly, the smallest packet of information (at the Planck scale) 'a bit' - also thought of as the smallest oscillation measurable (or packet of energy) - is known as a quantum. The quantum's energy varies, but every quantum contains the same value for angular momentum. Another term for angular momentum is action. Therefore the quantum field is a field of action and it's this field that our senses convert the vibratory electrical stimuli into what we consider to be the real world.

It's all a bit shady

Another interesting feedback loop is that of black and white. As we are aware black and white are not colours, they are shades. They are also considered opposite shades, but not the only shades. One more shade exists, that of grey. What we have is black at one end of the infinity symbol and white at the other. In between the two there are many more shades of grey than 50......ladies! The darkest shade of grey merging into black and becoming lighter until the lightest shade merges with white. It is important to understand that there are infinite shades of grey all relating to how the number system functions. What I mean by that is if we take a shade of grey and add a 0.01 tint of black it will darken it ever so slightly. We can do the same with 0.001 of tinting and so on ad infinitum. Hidden within the opposites of everything is infinity. Can you now appreciate the implications of this? Remember the mind is the process of deciding what something means within this feedback loop so therefore always has an infinity of choices. Can you now see why people can appear to you to be so irrational? They just see it from a different perspective and are making a different choice. There is no universal right and wrong, it's just that they have a different point of view. What you label right and wrong only applies to you from your personal point of view.

It's the devil in me

If we replace black and white with the analogy of darkness and light we can appreciate a little more how the opposites in the feedback loop require each other to exist in the mind. Note: A single unit or 'bit' of light is a photon and each photon 'appears to transport' a quantum of information. Therefore light is information and for that matter so is phonics (sound). Typically religious and spiritual mythology promotes stories of how the light defeats the darkness, but fails to show the eternal connection of the two. A typical story revolves around how no matter how dark a room is, a small candle can light up the room and defeat the darkness. What is quite often forgotten is there can be no light whatsoever, none at all, without the medium of darkness. For light to exist darkness must also exist. What is fascinating is to see how the law of opposites applies in this case.

"Look at how a single candle can both defy and define the darkness"

-Anne Frank

In the world from our point of view the light as we see it is enfolded within the darkness. Think about it, if the sun and the stars didn't shine there would be complete darkness. This suggests the universe we live in is a black hole and we as the observers are illuminating it from the inside. From this point of view, your outer reality is light enfolded within darkness. Let's imagine looking from the outside of a black hole. What we would see is total brightness as the event horizon is light on the circumference of a three dimensional sphere. Remember the blackhole as we tend to visualise it and see it on television is typically a two dimensional representation. It is a flat black circle surrounded by a circle of light at the circumference, but this is not accurate as we live in a three dimensional spacial reality. So our observations from the outside of a black hole looking in, is darkness completely surrounded by a light horizon, whereas within the black hole we are the light completely engulfed by the darkness. It is all about perspective. Of course when we are observing outside of the black hole we must be within a larger black hole for us to observe the light of the event horizon of the black hole we are observing. This is all a matter of scale and guess what? Must be infinite.

Photo courtesy of NASA

Now with total darkness being "infinite potential" having 'absorbed' all information, and light being the opposite 'the reflection of information', can you now begin to appreciate the eternal dance between the two? From infinite potential (spirit) the mind chooses (subjectively) to become something (objectively). This is an experience to which the mind attributes meaning (subjectively) concurrently informing (spirit) of this for the cycle to continue. This is the process of life and you are the boundary condition of your inner world (thoughts, feelings and emotions) to your outer world (objective reality). Take a moment, it's eternal anyway, to contemplate on what this really means.

CHAPTER 3

Science and Religion - two sides of the same coin

I grew up in an environment of Christian beliefs, overwhelmed by the British/Irish conflict, complicated by the Protestant/Catholic traditions. There were bombings, murder in the name of some belief labelled a cause and destruction on a large scale in a relatively small area of Northern Ireland. Of course it did filter out now and again to affect other areas that suffered widespread grief and devastation. This all in the name of labels. I am British, I am Protestant, I am Irish, I am Catholic. Fascinating to think that a large part of this conflict related to a hatred between two of the major Christian sects. The ironic part is the adherence to Catholicism or Protestantism that most who perpetrated these crimes claimed an affiliation to. Thou shall not kill springs to mind. Also the Jesus of the Christian bible taught two basic tenets; love God and love thy neighbour as thyself. In other words the latter meaning do not label or judge another. Northern

Ireland has a new found peace, for the most part. A few still harbour deep rooted feelings, wanting to drag the country back to the dark days, but on the whole most people have focused their energy in more productive pursuits.

Northern Ireland and the world have moved on...... to bigger and more devastating conflicts all in the name of labels linked to ideals......Yesterday Northern Ireland, today the Middle East. Yesterday Protestant versus Catholic, today Christian versus Muslim. Higher awareness allows you to see life's patterns. Evolution appears to be fractal in nature. A fractal is a self-repeating pattern at different scales. The next chapter goes into much more detail on this.

The Northern Ireland conflict is just one of many examples through the ages of where religious affiliation - and for that matter patriotism - binds a large percentage of people together, yet at the same time causes the same people to see others, who choose a different banner to associate with, as antagonists. Of the two, religion and patriotism, religion tends to evoke the stronger emotional feelings. People are much more accepting that you don't have much control over where you are born, but are aware that you have a choice in your religious beliefs even though for most it is a conditioning process. If you are brought up Catholic by your parents it's quite likely you'll accept Catholicism as your faith and pass onto your offspring. The church is well aware of this. You would have to be blind not to notice the fear tactics used in mental manipulation to keep you in the fold. Catholicism is just an example, it would appear to be the same for all the religious traditions. Ironically this is all carried out in the name of God who loves you - as long as......

The art of measurement

Let us turn our attention to Science and what it actually is. The word science comes from the Latin word 'Scientia' which means 'knowledge'. To attain this knowledge a process is adhered to, known as the scientific method. This process of inquiry is commonly based on empirical or measurable evidence based on natural phenomena subject to specific principles of reasoning. In other words the process of inquiry is commonly based on evidence of the senses (empirical) and mathematics (measurable). Current scientific thinking is immersed in two fundamental principles; materialism and reductionism. Materialism is the belief that the world 'out there' is made from particles of solid matter and reductionism is the belief that to understand how something works mechanically strip it to its base parts. Science bases its explanation on the results of experiments, objective evidence, and observable facts.

Before the advent of what's commonly termed western science, philosophy was generally considered the science of the day. Philosophy is the study of the fundamental nature of knowledge, reality and existence. Most of us have heard of Socrates, Plato, Aristotle and Archimedes from Greek Philosophy but there were many more philosophers throughout the ages from all over the world. Modern science differs from philosophy mainly through repeated trials of observable/measurable 'facts'.

The origins of the modern scientific revolution are rooted in the sixteenth century initially associated with Copernicus and then Galileo's belief, counter to the churches at the time, that the Earth moved around the Sun (heliocentric model). With the churches view being the opposite, putting the Earth at the centre of the universe, Galileo almost paid the ultimate price, but struck lucky and was only put under house arrest for the rest of his life! Apparently it was a nice house, spacious with built in study and fantastic views of the outside world.

Shortly after Galileo, Isaac Newton took the mantle, and pushed forward the mechanical nature of reality. Newton established classical equations which underpinned the industrial revolution amongst other things. His laws of motion and understanding of calculus lead to amazing technological advances even to this day. His Newtonian principles now referred to as classical physics formed the bedrock of the scientific method and by the end of the nineteenth century some scientists began to believe physics was on the verge of completion. Then...... BOOM!!!

The veil was lifted on the quantum world. What appeared to be the ending of one paradigm was the catalyst for the beginning of a whole new world. This world was stranger and more mysterious than anything ever encountered before. It was illogical, unpredictable, the opposite of common sense experiences and yet was the underpinning of everything that we knew. It is what everything appears to be made from.

Some of the early pioneers in the development of what has been later termed quantum theory, were people like Max Planck (often referred to as the father of quantum physics), Niels Bohr (the Copenhagen interpretation), Erwin Schrodinger (Schrodinger's cat), Werner Heisenberg (Heisenberg's uncertainty principle) and of course Albert Einstein. There were many more all aiding in the development of our modern day interpretation of the quantum world.

Quantum theory in simple terms is the science of the very small. The world of atoms and sub-atomic particles. In our macro world of objects such as trees, cars, bricks, air, water, even you and me, as well as all the space in between, are all composed of atoms and their sub-atomic particles. It is what everything, the seen and the unseen, are made from. Surprisingly, this level is so small that only the most powerful electron microscopes are able to view an atom. What is viewed is not an object however, but a map of electrical charge in the space where the atom resides. What is probably even more surprising is that the Greek philosophers around the 5th century BCE predicted the atom to exist as the basic building block of the universe.

Atom comes from the Greek word atomos which means indivisible. The atom to the ancient Greeks appeared to be the fundamental building block of all matter. From our modern day perspective it is astonishing that for their time they were able to come to this conclusion without the aid of the technology we have today at our disposal. Of course we now know the atom is divisible, containing a nucleus with protons and neutrons surrounded by an electron cloud of potential. The protons and neutrons can be further divided into quarks and gluons which turn out to be nothing more than waves of probability. The key word here is nothing (no-thing). As hard as it is for most to accept, due to their conditioning, the world we perceive is NOTHING!

With the advent of quantum physics which I will discuss in more detail in a later chapter we have been able to observe our reflection in the abyss of nothingness.

Yet from this nothingness comes mind, matter, space, time, energy and everything and anything imaginable.

> "Anyone who becomes seriously involved in the pursuit of science, becomes convinced, that there is a spirit manifest in the laws of the universe, a spirit vastly superior to that of man."

> -Albert Einstein

Western scientific thinking still finds it hard to let go of classical physics. The assumption the world is material, that matter is king, still prevails. To accept what the quantum world might be hinting at would take science back to the dark ages. You see, science hates faith. Faith is not measurable, it is not objective and cannot be touched by the senses.

> Faith is the substance of things hoped for, the evidence of things not yet seen.

> -Biblical reference

Many people involved in scientific pursuits claim to be atheists, but not all. The scientific community was left scarred by the church all those years ago and still harbours resentment. Scientists will go to great lengths to propose a matter based universe of chance. A universe devoid of an intelligent designer. A deity of chaos! The problem for science is new answers

John Ferris

tend to lead to a proliferation of more questions. It is quite common and comical to listen to a scientist wax lyrical about the excitement of new discoveries producing more questions than answers. It reminds me of the psychological drama of attempting to leave a room by moving half the distance each time you take a step. You basically end up going nowhere!

> "All matter originates and exists only by virtue of a force. We must assume behind this force is the existence of a conscious and intelligent mind. This mind is the matrix of all matter."
>
> -Max Planck

What Planck appears to be promoting is that objective reality, the world which our bodies inhabit and also our bodies themselves, appears to be created by unseen forces, a kind of mental illusion, of what we believe to be physical. This being the case, could it be our beliefs which are creating our reality? Also note how he uses the phrase 'we must assume' in other words faith. We must have faith that behind this force is a conscious and intelligent mind. He concludes with "this mind is the matrix of all matter", with a matrix being an environment in which something develops. A mental matrix can be thought of as a holographic reality.

In the movie 'The Matrix' there is a scene were Morpheus explains to Neo what the Matrix actually is. He uploads a computer programme in which he and Neo appear to exist. He explains that in this reality Neo's appearance is a residual self-image which is the mental projection of his digital self. In the programme there is a chair on which Neo places his hands and queries "this isn't real?" Morpheus's response is "what is real? How do you define real? If you are talking about what you can feel, what you can smell, what you can taste and see then real is simply electrical signals interpreted by your brain." As you can imagine Neo is totally confused. He is being asked to accept the matrix is a virtual reality programme which is something that goes completely against his lifetime of conditioning. His world view has been turned upside down.

The chair in question can be viewed from another perspective. Remember life's dual nature. There are always two sides to every story. Morpheus quite correctly described to Neo how we download information via electrical stimuli within the brain, but from the outer world perspective, what does science tell us about the chair? The chair from our point of view is an object believed to exist 'out there' in space and time and separate from ourselves. This is the common sense and classical physics point of view. Quantum physics tells us a completely different story. When we submerge ourselves within the quantum realm we see the chairs electrically charged atomic structure dissolve into protons, neutrons and electrons, then quarks and gluons before disappearing into a probability wave of potential. This leads us once more to the conclusion the chair at its fundamental level is nothing. Yet we can sit on the chair knowing, most likely, that it will hold our body weight......now that takes faith!

The measurement problem

Jesus told us all you need is the faith of a mustard seed. A mustard seed being the smallest seed known. He used this analogy to get the message across that faith is absolute. There is no difference between a lot of faith and a little faith. As I said before faith is unmeasurable, you either have faith or do not. Where does this faith originate? It originates in the realm of spirit or pure consciousness and you tap into it through your subconscious mind which is the orchestrator of your belief system. If you believe the chair to be stable in nature in all probability it will support your weight even though we have revealed it is made of nothing. Then again your body is also made from the same atomic structure as the chair which of course is nothing! Remember nothing is potential and you and the chair are both expressions (expressed outwardly) of this all governing potential.

So what does this tell us in relation to science and faith? As I see it, science, like religion and spirituality fundamentally is based on faith. Faith is built into the system, as is creativity, love, beauty etc. The subconscious mind would appear to be the connection of the egotistical you and Spirit. It acts as the conduit which passes through the mirror realities of the 'in here' and the 'out-there'.

The religious divide

Having provided a very brief synopsis of the history of science let's turn our attention to religion. One of the definitions of religion is to bind. In other words following a religious accord is a way of binding people together to follow a moral code of conduct and ethics. There are many religious traditions in the world, but probably the most referenced, in no particular order, are Christianity, Islam, Hinduism, Taoism, Judaism and Buddhism, although it is argued Buddhism is not a religion, but a way of life with no worship to a deity. With this in mind I include Buddhism loosely in the following argument due to it having a large following and a lot of people on the outside assuming it is a religion, but in many ways it is the opposite - at least from an exoteric point of view.

It is my belief that exoteric and esoteric are the keys to understanding the role of religion in society. From my experience and from conducting a straw poll the majority of people including those of a religious persuasion do not know what exoteric and esoteric, pertaining to religion, are, never mind the difference. This is important because they are opposites yet fall under one banner. Religion just like everything else including science (relativity and quantum) and you (inner world of thoughts, feelings and emotions and outer world of objects) is a feedback loop based on the law of opposites.

Exoteric religion in general is the rules, stipulations and dogma that separates one religion from the next. These are the boundary conditions each religion adds to keep you in the fold. To be a true Christian we are told we must be saved by the Lord Jesus Christ and the words contained in the bible are the word of God. Problem is at the last count there are 170 differing forms of Christianity all claiming theirs is the truth. The Christian Faith is based on the teachings of Jesus Christ, even though his surname is not Christ.....except in a fit of temper!!!

The term Christ comes from the Hebrew for Messiah or anointed one which is referencing his divinity through Christ consciousness. In the teachings that are attributed to Jesus he demonstrated this divinity. When I began my spiritual awakening I chose not to know about the birth and resurrection stories, I was just interested in what he said. When I googled this, up sprang the gospels of Thomas, yes, the doubting one as everyone tells me. To doubt is to question and surely there is nothing wrong with that. What struck me was the gospel of Thomas is omitted from the bible, yes......apparently because he doubted. Jesus says "If you want to throw the mountains into the sea, know without doubt and be thankful to God and it will be done for you", or words to that effect dependant on which of the myriad of bible translations you read. But to move mountains we must not doubt, guess what, we're all members of club Thomas. Point is, the gospels of Thomas are very compelling. When I read them, Jesus to me, spoke in a quantum/spiritual language which made sense. When you read it from an everyday, objective, common sense approach it reads like an LSD trip......man.

You see, according to many scholars the biblical stories are metaphors. The New Testament writers, Matthew, Mark, Luke, John, Paul and Ringo we're told, wrote the most well-known books at least one hundred years after the crucifixion of Jesus. If you think from an historical perspective you would expect when the *Chinese* got involved the *whispers* might have had some influence on the final draft, but maybe they had not yet crossed the Orient. It has been suggested that Matthew or Mark should have been disqualified as it's blatantly obvious one copied the other. Problem is, we don't know which one, so Constantine and his editors decided it was only fair to include both. Recorded history tells us this was in

325 AD some three hundred years later when the bible was put together.

Constantine was one of a quartet of Roman emperors, who got greedy. The Roman Empire had conquered a large part of Europe and some of Asia very successfully for many centuries using the template of four emperors. Constantine thought differently and figured it would work better if he had the lot. He conquered three quarters of the Roman Empire by denouncing his worship to the pagan Sun God and supposedly becoming a 'Christian'. This helped swell his manpower to overthrow two of the other emperors using Christians to fight on his behalf. When Byzantium fell he renamed it Constantinople (now Istanbul) in his honour and duly erected a statue of worship......to the Sun God. He did however oversee the origin of the Bible as we know it, or at least versions of the original. His editors, monks of the day, decided which books to include and which to omit. This is powerful stuff. To have the power to say what is 'truth' and what is 'not' for the masses to align to and convince them it is the word of God. I love the penultimate paragraph of revelations which threatens, anyone who adds to or removes any of the words contained within this book will be struck down by one of the plagues described herein......says God.

Really? Is our belief in this all powerful presence so small minded that God has to resort to threats and fear tactics to control people? If God is all knowing, everything and everywhere as the bible and the other religions tell us then what need for anything does God actually have? With this view it would suggest that God is impersonal. This I believe to be the case. A lot of scientists including Stephen Hawking struggle with a personal God that religions concoct. If God was viewed as impersonal then intelligent design might be more readily accepted by the scientific community. Potentially one half of the problem solved. OK religions, can this model bring you back on board? When we apply the feedback loop of the law of opposites we have God as the one whole spiritual essence of pure awareness being impersonal whilst simultaneously the infinite individuations of self-awareness that are all imbued with the same potential are personal.

I have referenced the Christian faith as my example because it is the religion I associate closest to in my model of reality. Closer inspection of the others fall along similar lines, but vary in their ritualistic nature and do's and don'ts. Exoteric is the outer part of religion which allows the few to control the belief systems of the many. For this to happen you must be prepared to give your power of freedom of choice away to another. Jesus pointed this out when he reflected on how they 'follow like sheep'.

Can't see the wood for the trees

It might come across that I am dead set against religion, I am not. We all have freedom to choose whatever, and each will extol its own benefits. Although I am not a member of any 'tribe' I do appreciate the need for humans to bind, but not to the detriment of those making a different choice. This is where religions tend to break down. This need to recruit is the catalyst for conflict. If all religions were able to drop their exoteric rules we would most certainly discover that underneath, hidden in the undergrowth, lies the esoteric form of religions which is the spiritual path. Jesus exclaimed "I am the way, the truth and the life". If you actually read without religious bias what is attributed to the sayings of Jesus it becomes quite obvious he is not a human being who existed 2000 years ago. He exists in you and it's your spirit (this is why he is known as the son of God), it's your inner divine wisdom that every one of us possesses that is the way, the truth and the life!

The esoteric form of religion, the Kabbalah in Judaism, the Upanishads in Hinduism, the Batini in Islam, is your inner spiritual nature which ironically all of the major religions fall into agreement with. They just word it differently, but ultimately tell the same story. In Christianity the Old Testament aligns more with an exoteric God of vengeance who composed Ten Commandments (laws) that you must abide by or suffer the consequences. In the New Testament God apparently embodied himself in man as Jesus and taught an esoteric form of religion (spirituality). He did away with the ten exoteric laws and replaced them with just two esoteric ones. Love God and love thy neighbour as thyself. In other words love everything as one. Jesus told us he lives within each and everyone of us and we must go through him to know God. When read correctly he is acknowledging our spirit within, not the misaligned exoteric teachings. The Buddha tells us that what you think you become - to follow the middle path with Krishna referring to each of us being infinite versions of self as one. Each one is saying the same thing dressed up differently. These are all tenets that fit an esoteric mould. An exoteric model is bounded and limited whereas an esoteric is the opposite, unbounded and unlimited.

I must take this opportunity to make the important point that Jesus was not a Christian. Christianity only formed many years later aligning itself (unfortunately somewhat vaguely with his teachings, most likely, due to the conflicting interpretations of the old and new testaments). He was apparently a Jew who obviously didn't practise. In simple terms he taught the Kingdom of heaven is inside each and every one of us. In essence the kingdom of heaven is not a location, it is a state of being or a state of divine consciousness which we can all exhibit. "I and the father are one and so are you", he told us. "You can do what I do and more". Jesus had demonstrated through his wonderful acts his spiritual connection and caught the attention of the people of his day. Problem is, it would appear the story of Jesus is……. just that, a story.

Only the awakened can know the truth

No authentic historical records of Jesus exist. Some might point to the shroud of Turin, but the funny thing is we have no idea what Jesus actually looked like. The depiction we have of a white man with a beard was Leonardo Da Vinci's interpretation and has since caught on and been passed down as…...gospel! The story of the virgin birth on December 25th, the star in the east, adored by three kings, twelve disciples, performing miracles, crucified and resurrected after three days amongst others has been told throughout the ages by many different cultures. These attributes can be related to many other gods who have the same mythological structure such as Horus the Egyptian sun god around 3000 BC, Mithra of Persia 1200 BC, Krishna of India 900 BC, Dionysus of Greece 500 BC and many others. The question then is how can so many cultures at different times in history come up with such a similar story? Could it be that all of these stories relating to the son of God are actually about the sun of God? Astrologically Dec 25th is the birth of the winter solstice and on Dec 24th the brightest star in the night sky is Sirius (the star in the east) which aligns precisely with the three stars of Orion's belt (the three kings) and all point to where the sun rises on Dec 25th at some point during that day. This I am led to believe is always the case no matter what year it is, therefore cultures from different places at different times astrologically will see the same thing in the night sky, I must add this all takes place from a northern hemisphere perspective. Next question you might ask is how did they come up with such similar stories? The hundredth monkey effect is a scientifically studied phenomenon. According to Wikipedia it is when a new behaviour or idea is claimed to spread rapidly by unexplained means from one group to another, irrespective of period and location, once a critical number of members of one group exhibit the new behaviour or acknowledge the new idea. This being the case it would help explain how this particular allegory has perpetuated throughout the 'human psyche'.

People of the Christian Faith who are hearing this for the first time might be abhorred by this revelation. To some it is apocalyptic. I say this because back in the time the bible was written the word apocalypse had a different meaning than it has today. In today's world an apocalyptic event is an end of the world scenario. Back in the day of the scripture writer's apocalypse meant 'revelation' (to reveal) or 'secret knowledge'. Even a lot of the modern dictionaries have not realised this. Chinese whispers in our time crossed the orient long ago. Realisations like this can throw a completely different complexion on things. In one case we're all going to die, in the other we're all going to evolve. You choose!

A lot of people will not allow themselves to believe such nonsense. In their defence this is typically normal human behaviour. As human beings we create our world view through the meaning we put to the sum total of our environmental experiences and then defend it to the hilt. Your defences only crack when you choose to allow new ideas to flourish and this will be dependent on how open minded you are. Hardened sceptics rarely change no matter how much evidence you put before them, but this is their divine right also. Who am I or anyone else to force opinions down other's throats? All I am attempting to do is encourage you to question, to allow for a more unbounded and less dogmatic view of the world and of existence itself.

Know the truth and the truth shall make you free we are told. What if from your point of view there is no universal truth? What if there was only your truth as the creator of your story and everyone else's truth as the creator of their stories, guided paradoxically by a few divine laws. This model of reality would answer the question to why there exists so much conflict. It would also reveal to you why so many global institutions would not want you to know this. Once this truth becomes mainstream, control, greed and manipulation fade into oblivion and slavery once and for all is truly abolished.

"None are more hopelessly enslaved than those who falsely believe they are free"

-Goethe

Science is religion spelt backwards

To conclude, I began this chapter claiming science and religion are two sides of the same coin. Robert Jastrow an agnostic world renowned astronomer on the scientific discovery of the Big Bang concluded "there is a kind of religion in science. It is the religion of a person who believes there is order and harmony in the Universe. This religious faith of the scientist is violated by the discovery that the world had a beginning under conditions in which the known laws of physics are not valid, and as a product of forces or circumstances we cannot discover. When that happens, the scientist has lost control. If he really examined the implications, he would be traumatised."

Science, just like religion, binds people together as believers in a dogmatic fashion. The scientific way, the scientific truth and the scientific life. Both science and religion as I've shown require faith as part of their belief systems. They both have specific guidelines that must be adhered to. If you do not adhere and you step outside these parameters you are seen as a heretic, ridiculed and cast adrift from the flock. In the case of science I am referring to the scientists themselves whose funding gets cut or stopped completely. Finally, mainstream science like all religions is bounded and constrained in its pursuit of truth by man-made principles and assumptions that do not cater to the opposite approach and basically ignore and deflect, just like an adeptly trained politician, any notion other than its own belief. But to me the biggest nail in the scientific mainstreams coffin is the ignorance of consciousness. The standard model has no place for consciousness.

> A problem cannot be resolved at the level it was created
>
> -Albert Einstein

Science and scientists have achieved wonderful scientific advances which I applaud them for, but when it comes to answering the fundamental questions of who you are and how it all began it flounders in the wind. Like a ship without a rudder it floats about on the high seas hoping to find a destination as long as it's not dry land. No single methodology can have all the answers to life's ultimate questions. The infinite cannot be bound by any religious or scientific model. The spiritual path is not a methodology as it's all encompassing. Yet to know infinity is futile as infinity itself is all knowing and we are entwined within this knowingness, but that does not prevent us from understanding the principles, purpose and patterns behind the infinite.

CHAPTER 4

The Hidden Patterns of Reality

Let's examine some principles and methodology that allow infinity to flourish. Looking through the eyes of the current mode of scientific thinking, the standard model in physics, as well as those of all religious persuasions, we realise they are all subsets of a larger system. Anything that is exclusive in nature can only be a part of a larger whole. This is a key point in people's understanding that tends to be overlooked. Dogmatism is the culprit. It is an extremely powerful human trait that few overcome.

This does not conclude that either path, be it science or religion, cannot help enlighten us to the bigger picture. Both have the ability to do so, but in so doing ultimately merge into one spiritual path. Every path eventually leads you home. There is nowhere else for it to go. It's just that the modern scientific mode of thinking and the numerous religious accords erect enormous walls around their perimeters and a circular thought pattern takes over. The boundary condition creates a sense of safety whilst imprisoning our thoughts and keeping them from venturing into a world where confusion reigns. "Stick with the current paradigm!" our ego screams, "people will accept me more for who I am", whilst at the same time a yearning is always subtly knocking on the door, waiting for it to be opened to reveal you are more than your ego - much, much more! This circular thought pattern is a two dimensional approach. Think about it. All circles are two dimensional. We do not live in a two dimensional world, we live in a three dimensional world. A three dimensional circle is a sphere, but when you include the fourth dimension of time the perception of movement occurs. A good analogy for this is our solar system.

If it's repeated often enough then it must be true

The heliocentric principle taught in school is the latest 'metaphor' for how the solar system functions. I will explain why I use the term metaphor in the final chapter. We are generally taught that the planets orbit the sun in an elliptical manner with the sun remaining stationary at the centre. If that were the case, and accepting it's the mass of the sun that holds the whole system together, then what is holding the sun in place? You see, in physics nothing is stationary, everything has angular momentum, nothing is in the same position as it was a moment ago - and that includes the sun. A correlation exists between change and the addition of new information. If the planets in our solar system rotated the way it is generally envisaged - in a circular pattern around the sun - each full rotation would cause the same information to be experienced (an observer must be present for the perception of time) over and over again. So, if it took one year to circumnavigate, the observer would experience the same year repeatedly. Groundhog year can be overcome by visualising the planets moving around the sun in a spiral formation with the sun spiralling around the galactic centre and the galactic centre spiralling around the galactic cluster and so on. Is it any wonder your head's in a spin! Paradoxically stillness is the accumulation of all spin; this is one reason why our everyday perception of reality appears relatively still, the other being that movement is a series of stills, but that's another discussion. We seem to experience time moving in only one direction, but is this wholly true? What is the experience we have if this forward momentum is reversed?......it is called a memory. A memory is the retrieval of past information. Would it surprise you to know that studies have shown that the same memory never contains the exact same information? It's your ego that recalls the past and imagines the future. Both past and future are imagined events always open to new information. They are imaged into action by your mind. The observer only exists in the present. It is only the observer who is having the experience.

In physics we are told there is no apparent reason why time appears to flow in one direction only. There are no laws to say time cannot flow backwards. The forward direction of time comes about from our sensory perspective of the world, but this is only an assumption. When you wake up in the morning you assume that when you elicit a memory of yesterday, that it actually happened yesterday - but this is unprovable. Even though you might say I can get someone else to verify this, the verification still comes about from your own point of view, and is therefore rendered meaningless. As previously discussed, time is not what we think it is. We create our personal time in our personal reality tunnel from our personal point of view to differentiate our personal experiences. Time is personal! Infinity is not! Infinity (impersonal) is the observer of itself through you (personal), projecting a finite boundary to differentiate the observed, with each observation occurring within the illusion of time. To envisage this, a three dimensional geometrical pattern that caters for open loop evolution within a boundary condition that expands and contracts is required. Basically an upgrade of the infinity symbol.

The Torus

This pattern is the torus structure. Think of a doughnut shape with a small hole in the middle. It is a dynamic energy pattern that can sustain itself whilst being made from the same substance as its surroundings. Think of water going down a drain which has a vorticular motion with two directions of rotation, horizontal and vertical. When we incorporate a double torus one on top of the other, with a singularity in the middle, balance is achieved at this still point. It is an infinitely evolving expansive and contractive system embracing polar opposites as complementary.

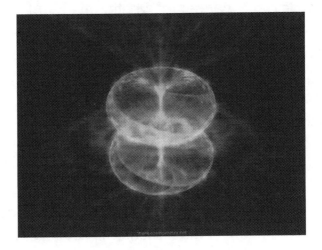

According to scientific philosophers Arthur Eddington and Arthur M Young, the torus dynamic is the pattern which unifies general relativity with quantum physics. Without delving into the mathematics, Eddington equated the curvature of spacetime with the curvature of uncertainty. To achieve this a self sustaining energetic information pattern was required that could be applied at all scales from the very smallest, the photon, to the largest, the universe and everything in between. This included stars, planets, atoms as well as trees, plants, tornadoes - even you and me.

The toroidal structure is this pattern. It can exchange energy and information seamlessly embedded fractally at all scales. One dynamic, one system....... oneness.

> "The self in a toroidal universe can be both separate and connected with everything else"

> -Arthur M Young

The earth exhibits the traits of a double torus pattern. If you look at the weather systems in the northern hemisphere you will see they rotate in the opposite direction to those in the southern hemisphere, while both move from the equator towards the polar regions. Water flowing down a drain is another example of this with it being counter clockwise above the equator and clockwise below.

The law of opposites feedback loop, based on the power of three, is beautifully imagined through the double torus system. On a side note, for all the physics buffs, I believe the Dirac equation - which is considered one of the most beautiful equations in all of physics - is connected to this principle. Paul Dirac in 1933 won the Nobel prize in physics for his theory that combined quantum mechanics with special relativity. His equation explains the behaviour of matter at the sub-atomic level and how it relates to light. It was the first time something never before seen in nature was predicted to exist. It didn't end there though. The equation also predicted the existence of the mirror universe of antimatter.

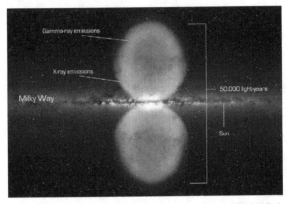

Photo courtesy of NASA

Think of the above torus as the universe we live in made from matter with its mirror torus below made from antimatter. As above so below........for all the religious buffs, with the spiritual still point residing at the centre for balance and equilibrium. Science at one end, religion the other, all being pulled by spiritual strings.

Due to the torus structure being infinite in nature, by default, the expansion and contraction (when we add meaning) of information must also be infinite. The generator of this infinite amount of information is the singularity. Remember the singularity is the void of infinite potential, where out of nothingness comes everything. For this to function a model is required that can contain infinite information. Do we know of such a model? Absolutely. It is the holofractographic model, which is a hologram embedded in a fractal system and it fits just like a glove.

What is a Hologram?

The theory of holograms was first proposed in 1947 by Dennis Gabor whilst working on the electron microscope to improve its resolution, but it wasn't until 1960 with the invention of the laser that holography really took off. It was Gabor who coined the phrase hologram from the Greek words holos meaning "whole" and gramma meaning "message".

A hologram is produced by a single laser light which is split into two by what is known as a beam splitter. An interference pattern is recorded on film by one beam bouncing off the object in question and the second beam colliding with the light of the first. This interference pattern is a 2D wavelike image which to the human brain is meaningless, but the magic happens when this film is illuminated by another laser and a 3D representation of the object in question appears. Take note: the two dimensional interference pattern is crucial to the holographic projection.

What is truly startling about this image is instead of it being constructed by individual parts making up a whole (what we perceive in everyday reality), every aspect is a smaller version of the whole thing. In simple terms all of the information of the 'whole' is present everywhere (omnipresence). If our holographic film is cut in two and we shine the laser on either/or, we still have the whole object on each film. We can cut the film into as many pieces as we choose and no matter which one we illuminate we always have the whole object. This is because light from every point on the object is captured at every point on the holographic film. Therefore what is most important to know is that every individual point in the hologram holds all the information of the whole hologram. Remember light is information (each photon of light equates to a single 'bit' of information). It must be noted that the smaller the piece of film when cut from the original that is illuminated the fuzzier the hologram becomes. To some this is considered loss of information. I don't think so. Welcome to fractals!

What is a fractal?

A fractal is a never ending pattern that is self similar across all scales. Fractals are created by a simple repeating process, recursion, within a feedback loop system. Therefore fractality can be viewed as a model that embeds all information (omnipresence). Infinity resides within every boundary condition through fractality.

Fractal patterns are everywhere in nature. Look down and you will see them in the grass and plants, look up and you see them in clouds and weather patterns, look down when you're up and you see them in rivers and coastlines, look all around and you will see them in trees and mountain ranges. Everywhere you look you will find them. Think of a fractal this way. If you were able to remove a small portion of a cloud from a larger cloud it would look self similar. Take a branch from a tree and you will see the same pattern as the whole tree at a smaller scale. Some things are not as obvious, but if you look deeply enough into anything you will discover this repeat pattern. It is all about perspective.

To appreciate how a fractal pattern originates from simple laws let's look at the most famous computer generated fractal of all, the Mandelbrot Set. Produced by the Polish born French mathematician Benoit

Mandelbrot this complex infinite fractal pattern was derived from the simple equation $Z = Z^2 + C$. Check out the Mandlebrot set on a computer to appreciate fully.

As above so below, I believe, is referencing the fractal nature of the Universe and beyond. The largest thing we can measure is the diameter of the observable universe which is approximately 93 billion light years across. The universe has not existed long enough to measure light beyond this boundary condition, or at least that is the assumption. The smallest thing we can measure is the Planck length which is the smallest wavelength of the electromagnetic spectrum 1.616×10^{-35} cm, also light in the guise of a photon. The Planck scale is the inner boundary condition known as the vacuum density or zero point field. Each Planck is spherical in shape and oscillates at a particular frequency carrying a single bit of information. To say it is very small is an understatement. Note how the topology of the observable universe and the Planck oscillation are both spherical. It has been calculated that a 0.1mm diameter sphere would be halfway in scale between the observable universe and the Planck. More proof that biology is at the centre of the universe and fractals are fundamental to this.

Fractals are also linked to the golden mean ratio of 1:1.618 which is the perfect compression spiral ratio. Note: A Planck oscillation is measured at 1.616×10^{-35}

cm. It is well within the margin of error to accept that each Planck oscillation is related in some way to the golden mean ratio. Nassim Haramein realised that Gravity is a geometric ratio between the number of Planck vacuum oscillations on the holographic surface horizon to the amount contained in the volume of a black hole. This produces a spinning dynamic in the form of a torsion curling effect leading to compression (like water going down a drain). This is gravitation. From this we can conclude the force of gravity is the electromagnetic force in reverse.

With the golden mean ratio being the perfect compression spiral (gravitation) its mirror image would be the imperfect Fibonacci sequence (electromagnetic radiation) related to life. This imperfection caters for infinite variety.

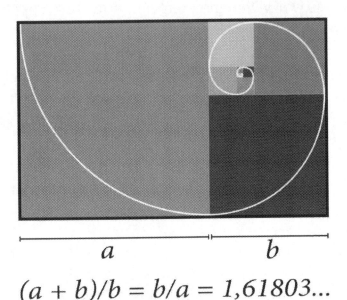

$$(a + b)/b = b/a = 1,61803...$$

Fractals are far more prominent than most people realise. How do you insert two metres of DNA in every minuscule cell within the human body without getting tangled? By fractal geometry! How do you squeeze into the human body miles and miles of blood vessels and capillaries? You guessed it, by fractality. From the ecosystem and living organisms to synthetic systems and even the synoptic system in the human brain, all exhibit a fractal nature. It is the perfect way of inserting the large into the very small as well as being extremely economical in the process.

"Fractality is perfect compression. Infinite non-destructive compression creates the possibility of perfect charge distribution which is life"

-Dan Winter

The Heart and Brain

Life being the distribution of charge must relate to the electromagnetic spectrum. Your body requires a model in which the electromagnetic signals can be received, decoded and transmitted. The models key components are the heart and brain.

I find it staggering that in the 21st Century neuroscience, psychology, psychiatry and biology still do not know the difference between brain and mind. Commonly doctors, scientists and people in general reference the brain and the mind as the same thing. I am utterly convinced this is not, and cannot be, the case. It's a bit like saying your eye and your sight are the same thing. Obviously they are not, although a close relationship does exist. The brain has never, and will never have a thought in its life. A brain does not think. That is not what it's for.

"Looking for consciousness in the brain is like looking inside a radio for the announcer"

-Nassim Haramein

The brain is a transmitter/receiver of information. It is an organ just like your liver, kidneys or pancreas, and comes in second only to the heart in the hierarchical system of your everyday functioning. Research conducted by the Heartmath institute and others have concluded that the heart carries out far more functions than just acting as a simple pump. To quote "the heart is in fact, a highly complex, self organised information processing centre with its own functional 'brain' that communicates with and influences the cranial brain via the nervous system, hormonal system and other pathways. These influences profoundly affect brain function and most of the bodies major organs and ultimately determine the quality of life".

Studies have suggested that the heart responds prior to brain response from environmental stimulation. This in itself is quite extraordinary due to it not being common knowledge, but what is even more intriguing is that the responses of both the heart and the brain take place before the event in question. In other words, the heart has prior knowledge of future events and then informs the brain. Only after the brain receives this information does the circumstance occur. This is incredible information. According to the Heartmath institute this is all verifiable. It appears the heart and brain have access to a field of information not bound by space and time. This backs up the belief that you are the creator of space and time. Space and time are mental constructs within which you create your experience of reality. Each one of us creates our own personal reality tunnel within which we experience life, but the paradox arises due to how your reality tunnel interferes with everyone else's reality tunnel that you come into contact with. Remember an interference pattern is required to produce a holographic reality.

Both the heart and the brain require an electrical circuit to function which always produces a magnetic field. The hearts magnetic field is by far the strongest produced by the human body. When the heart stops out come the jump leads to restart. It would appear the field of information not bound by space and time is the electromagnetic field. This being the case (I will discuss more in the next chapter) creates a paradox. The paradox is that everything in our space and time reality tunnel where we have our experiences is the electromagnetic field. So the only conclusion that can be drawn is that the electromagnetic field exists outside of space and time, but is also what space and time is composed off. This is life Jim, but not as we know it!

The heart has always been associated with the emotion of love whilst the brain is associated with the mind. With your thoughts being localised or decoded within your brain, it would give the impression that thoughts originate in the brain. This is not the case. Thoughts originate from the source of the signal, the heart and brain receive and transmit as your everyday experience of reality. This process is the relationship with the mind.

Some people might assume an MRI image, showing a region of the brain lighting up when a thought is elicited, as proof that the brain is thinking. This is like saying a footprint in the sand is a foot. What we are actually seeing is the region of the brain which receives and then transmits the information via the electrical impulses across the synapses. The brain (quantum) can be likened to a transistor radio (digital) that houses the electrical circuitry, but only functions when it is switched on and tuned to a specific frequency.

> "If the brain is the radio's receiver then the heart is the dial tuning the radio to the frequency of your choice"
>
> -Nassim Haramein

From a field of infinite possibilities you generate a signal of intention related to your focus of attention (consciously or subconsciously) by tuning into electrical frequencies with your heart, which your brain then decodes. Your brain transmits holographically what you perceive as a localised spacetime reality. Your body, heart and brain are included within this 'environmental' holographic field to allow your heart to imprint your emotional status into the magnetic field and the brain to process what it means into the electrical field. The environment within which the people, places, circumstances and events take place is the electromagnetic radiation, with gravity acting as its feedback counterpart to inform the vacuum density or zero point field.

Another linguistic clue pops up in the word environmental. Synonyms for 'environ' are to encircle or to encompass with 'mental' being the mind. This gives us another clue that the environment we perceive is a construct of the mind. In simple language your heart, brain, body, people, trees, water, stars, universe and everything that you imagine is all a part of a greater imagination of a cosmic mind expressing waves of potential and being localised by you as a physical experience. Through your sensory awareness you then feed back what you think and feel about the experience to your fundamental source.

> "You are not in the Universe, the Universe is in you"
>
> -Deepak Chopra

The universe is being created by and through you while paradoxically it's also a collective collaboration. You are a co-creator along with the sum total of all the other co-creators we acknowledge as God (spirit). Once again it's the paradox of the one and the many.

However, the question still arises "how can the brain perform the amazing feats it does?" If I am correct and the brain is involved in projecting a four dimensional holographic reality in which we interact with, as our world of experience, it then follows the brain must be a three dimensional hologram constructed from a two dimensional holographic image. But not just holographic it must also operate fractally.

Karl Pribram, a prominent neuroscientist, spent a large part of his working life along with others, showing how the brain stores information holographically which he called the holonomic brain theory. Also quite recently in 2012 Wai H Sang proposed his version of the fractal brain theory. Both theories would appear compatible with each other, but I will let you decide. With the Internet, YouTube and social media easily accessible today, it provides us all with the opportunity to survey vast amounts of information for clarification quickly and effectively.

The holographic fractal theory or holofractographic theory (coined by Nassim Haramein) has grown in recent years due to its ability to pull together the inner and outer worlds and unify in a relatively straightforward manner the unified field theory of everything. Many people agree that it's beauty is in it's simplicity.

"Truth is ever to be found in simplicity,
and not in the multiplicity and confusion
of things"

-Isaac Newton

CHAPTER 5

The Holofractographic Theory

Science and scientific research play a massive role in modern society. A lot of it is for the greater good for which we are all thankful, but some of it is destructive and can be misleading. The development of weapons and bombs is very much on the destructive side, but my concern is more to do with how science can mislead us in so many ways in order to convince us that the universe can exist without us and how insignificant we are within the vastness of that universe. This mainstream opinion would appear as self evident to many. How could we as human beings inhabiting a tiny speck in space and time have any real influence when it comes to something as large as the universe? Yes, we can affect our local surroundings somewhat, but generally it would appear negligible when you consider the scale of the universe. Once again we can apply the paradox that is the feedback loop, based on the law of opposites, to you and the universe. Mainstream science views it from the universal perspective and common sense would appear to back that stance up, but as we now know both you and the universe are intimately connected and when viewed from your point of view something incredible comes to light.

The Paradigm Shift

Classical Newtonian physics of a mechanistic clockwork universe held sway for hundreds of years. The calculations seemed to work for the scale of the billiard ball and galactic orbits. Newtons laws of motion and universal gravitational principles were the bedrock for his publication "Mathematical Principles of Natural Philosophy". Everything appeared rosy in the garden or so it seemed and then Rosy got up and left.

The first serious cracks started to appear in the nineteenth century when Scottish scientist James Clerk Maxwell formulated his classical theory of electromagnetic radiation which was to become known as electromagnetism or the electromagnetic field theory. The electromagnetic spectrum is the field which you interpret as everyday reality. A field in physics terms is a 'physical' quantity associated with every point of spacetime. Physics is still taught in this way due to the assumption the world 'out there' is solid in nature and exists whether or not a conscious observer is present. This goes against everything the quantum world is telling us. In fact this 'physical' quantity is brought about by unseen forces, that travel in waves at the speed of light, which exist everywhere. A field is non physical, but from which the physical appears to manifest. Therefore a field is metaphysical. Just a single charged particle creates an electric field everywhere throughout the entire universe. How many people are aware of this? This is mainstream science's view yet the interpretation and what is broadcast to the masses does not fit with the science. We are told we are insignificant in the vastness of the universe, yet the same sources peddling this misinformation tell us discreetly how a single particle of charge exists everywhere in the entire universe. Think about what is being said, this is so important. A single charge and the whole electromagnetic field are one and the same at a more fundamental level.

Maxwell postulated electricity, magnetism and light were all manifestations of the same phenomenon. This realisation is one of the greatest achievements in physics. However, though only really acknowledged at the superficial level, it is possibly one of the most brushed-under-the-carpet discoveries at a deeper level. Once again we have a play on opposites going on. The interconnectedness of the trinity of electricity, magnetism and light paved the way for field theory to be the underlying cause of the manifestation of particles. Every electric current creates a magnetic field and every magnetic field creates an electric current with both travelling in waves at the speed of light. The universe that we experience is composed from the electromagnetic spectrum, unseen forces travelling as waves at light speed creating perturbations within this field that we, as conscious observers, interpret as objects. The formless becomes form. Materialists dress it up differently, the awakened remove the veil.

Einstein's general relativity was published 11 years after his special relativity rocked science to its core knocking Newton of his pedestal, well sort of...... eventually. Newtonian physics is the study of the motion of bodies subject to the action of forces which describe a set of physical laws. Newtonian physics sometimes referred to as classical mechanics describes the world at the macroscopic level. This is the level we perceive objectively as cars, planes, planets, stars and galaxies. It also deals with liquids and gases. The Newtonian approach is very mechanistic and clockwork in nature and tends to equate with our common sense perception of the world. Time is constant no matter where you are in the universe and how fast you are travelling. Look at a clock and watch the seconds tick by at the same rate for everyone. This belief held true for hundreds of years until a patent clerk with a very vivid imagination turned everything on its head.

The patent clerk in question was Albert Einstein who had failed some of his early school exams resenting the schools regime and teaching methods. The man who later became the hero to most of the prominent scientists alive today wasn't officially qualified as a 'scientist' when his papers on special relativity and the photo electric effect amongst others were published. His efforts were recognised soon after by the University of Zurich and in 1905 he was awarded a PhD. The likelihood is, if he were alive today and took the same path, he would probably be mocked and ridiculed due to not following the accepted schooling channels. Yet the irony is if he had been schooled in the normal way he might not have thought outside of the box and come up with his amazing ideas. Of course Einstein's paper on special relativity did not catch on for many years as science by its very nature is extremely slow to change. The status quo is always maintained until an overwhelming amount of evidence suggests otherwise or the old guard fade away. Einstein was greatly helped at the time by the advances in the quantum world which mirrored to a high degree his theories on relativity in a weird and wonderful way.

It's all relative or is it?

Einstein's belief was that the speed of light set the universal speed limit; that 'information' between two points could not travel any faster, 186,200 miles per second in the vacuum of space to be precise. He also realised light speed is absolute. In other words if you are observing a photon it will always be travelling at 186,202 miles per second from your perspective no matter how fast you are travelling and in whatever direction. He imagined riding on a photon, the smallest quantised packet of information, travelling at the speed of light and questioned what he would see in front of him - with the conclusion being quite staggering. From another observers perspective the closer Einstein got to travelling at light speed the more time would slow down (dilate) and the more space would appear compressed. If Einstein managed to climb aboard the photon, time and space would completely vanish. Einstein realised nothing exists in the space ahead of or prior to the photon...........absolutely no-thing! Light in effect is actually motionless. It exists in a domain outside of our perspective of space and time yet paradoxically we observe it always having an absolute speed within the frame of reference of the reality tunnel we construct. Quantum theory backed this up even further when it labeled light a 'ghost' particle suggesting that the photons of light themselves were massless, yet to be able to travel at light speed it would theoretically require an infinite amount of energy. Ironically, one of Einstein's greatest contributions was the the formula $E - MC^2$. Everything in the universe is energy in some form, with energy and mass being interchangeable, as they are the same thing. I sense a paradox. In the quantum world we are told light has no mass, yet in the objective world it requires an infinite amount of energy to travel at light speed.

So what is light? Is it a wave or a particle? It appears in certain cases to act as a wave, but in others the photons appear as discrete particles. If we apply the principle of the law of opposites based on the power of three we can conclude, by accepting light comes in only two forms, wave or particle, they are opposites. A wave is spread out in a field system with light at every point, whereas particles have definite locations in space and time. The critical question we must ask is, "what connects the two?" Even before we explain in detail probably the most famous experiment in quantum physics, we can logically deduce that to know whether light is acting as a wave or a particle, a self-aware conscious observer must be present to ask the question in the first place. This is primary! Can light exist without an observer or anything for that matter? That which is known requires a knower, and the process of knowing, therefore I think not. To think requires a mind, and mind can only exist as dual nature, with duality requiring the space in between. Even from this point of view, being a sub-system of the whole, the appreciation of the twofold process based on the power of three is the fundamental principle of THE SYSTEM. What is staring us straight in the face is YOU as the observer must be built into the system for the system to function. Without you there is no system. John Archibald Wheeler, a protégé of Einstein concluded we are participators in a participatory universe. Without us, no universe. This by many will be seen as a philosophical view, not scientific. So what? Remember the scientific method is a subset itself, a model, of the whole system, but here's the kicker - it's also a subset of YOU. Who was it who decided the scientific method? We did! When we delve into the quantum world we discover the experimenter, and/or the interpreter of the results, bias is always at play. You are entangled within the whole system. Try as we may, even through double blind experiments, our bias is always lurking in the background. Every time we think we have established the facts, given time, the facts change or in some cases appear to totally disappear, just like light.

To see or not to see

The double slit experiment in quantum physics has baffled many of the best scientific minds, but not those who are not weighed down by toeing the party line. From a certain perspective the conclusions are blatantly obvious, from another it's considered hocus pocus. Where is the boundary between science and mysticism? Does a boundary actually exist? If it does who put it there?

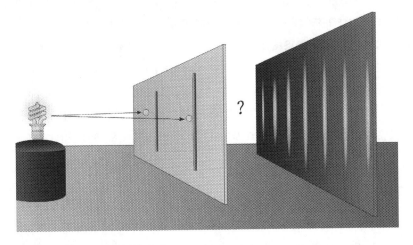

May I be so bold as to speak for the mainstream scientific community? The general consensus appears to be that the boundary between science and mysticism begins as soon as things become counterintuitive (paradoxical), therefore just ignore or act in a dogmatic way and play dumb. Believe with the utmost 'faith' that, of course, a boundary exists and do not question what these mystic arts may be, as this is considered heresy......it is not scientific! Of course, the boundary is put there by us, due to the belief the scientific method is the only way!

When we accept that no boundary actually exists between what science - more accurately quantum physics - is telling us, and mysticism - more accurately spirituality - progress can be made. The conclusions from the quantum double slit experiment that can be established with an open mind are, and were by many physicists, earth shattering. In a nutshell, we discovered matter can act like a wave (wave of potential) as well as a particle (solidity), with the determining factor being you. You, as the observer of the experiment, are what is determining the outcome. In physics language it is you who 'collapses the wave function' into what we interpret as a material concrete world. The wave function is a mathematical formula that basically says a particle is spread out everywhere at once (field), in what's known as superposition, with the possibility of having many different characteristics until an observer collapses this into a definite position with definite characteristics. We non physicists refer to this as everyday reality. Correct me if I'm wrong, but if a particle exists everywhere at the same time before we observe it, that sounds to me like omnipresence - and if the observer has the power - through the act of measurement - to create their own reality tunnel it suggests omnipotence. Imagine when creating your reality tunnel you were remembering, putting together parts of what you already know, would that be omniscience? Now let's not jump to any conclusions just yet, heavens above, who do you think you are!

It's dark out there

The standard model of cosmology, the Big Bang theory, has a massive problem with the force of gravity. We understand how gravity appears to work at a human level, take a bow Mr. Newton. Einstein's field equations - which form the basis of general relativity - give us an appreciation of the topology of the curvature of spacetime, and how objects move relative to each other. All well and good, except there is just not enough of the damn stuff to hold galaxies together. On top of that no-one has produced a creditable or acceptable theory of how to merge relativistic theory (the theory of the very large, the macro-verse) and quantum mechanics (the theory of the very small, the micro-verse) into a unified theory of everything. In simple terms, scientists do not know what gravity is. They understand what it appears to do but it is inconsistent at different scales. Gravity within the standard model is just too weak. At the universal level it appears as an extremely weak force. This turns out to be very intriguing and we will address this shortly. When problems of this nature arise scientists tend to fudge it by dogmatically sticking to the original theory and coming up with a new force, in this case dark matter. They assign it a mathematical value or percentage and then spend millions trying to find proof. This might be acceptable if only a few problems were encountered, but I read recently that the standard model has around thirty major discrepancies. We are told dark matter is the same as the matter we can see, except it does not contain a light signature, has no information attributed to it, and can pass straight through you whilst being undetectable. Is it possible science is living in the dark ages and has yet to see the light?

Full steam ahead no matter what

The standard model can only account for approximately 3% of the universe. The other 97% is made up of unseen forces, that of dark matter and a more recent addition - dark energy. Once again dark being the operative word, as it's seemingly undetectable. Around 73% of our universe consists of this mysterious expansive force, which is pushing the galaxies further and further apart at an ever increasing rate. If I only got 3% in my physics test I think I would take the time to self-reflect and revise my methods. On a side note I find it interesting that the visible light spectrum on the electromagnetic scale accounts for approximately 3%! Also psychologists attribute the conscious mind to operate at around 3% whilst the subconscious accounts for the rest and the functional protein encoding DNA is also in the region of 3% whilst science until recently considered the other 97% junk, apparently a mistake of nature. Absolute nonsense! Check out the work of Fritz Albert Pop, who in the 1980's discovered biophoton and biophonon communication of DNA, which, for whatever reason, has been suppressed by the powers that be. I wonder, if a correlation exists between all of the above and is it possible they could be one and the same, manifesting under different guises?

John Ferris

Star Wars: A New Hope

It's all well and good being able to find fault in others work, but if you're not prepared to offer a workable alternative then what is the point? The real fun is being able to supersede a theory with one that ticks all the boxes. Step forward the holofractographic universe theory. This theory has been proposed in recent years by Nassim Haramein of the Resonance Project who, by pulling together the work of many individuals over many decades, hopes to convince the mainstream view that this is a more viable alternative to the standard model. In so doing it also ties in with esoteric spiritual wisdom to allow for a much greater inclusive unified theory of everything.

The holofractographic theory is a field theory that unifies the very large (relativistic theory) with the very small (quantum theory), something Einstein - and now the standard model in science - has thus far failed to do with gravity proving a real sticking point. It shows the non-linear interconnectivity of all things - everything spins. It provides scientific evidence that everything is one which merges science with spirituality. It advances science to a holistic level to allow consciousness (spirit) to re-enter the picture as the ground state of being. It does this by reducing the materialistic solid world to a world of potentials - arising from nothing to become something - subjectively experienced holographically extending to infinity in both directions in a fractal series. The theory proposes the universe is composed of singularities at the core of all things. From the largest to the smallest every thing is connected fractally by singularities which exist at the centre of black wholes. Singularities are infinitely dense regions or points in space that curve light around the perimeter known as the event horizon which manifests as a black whole. Everything in existence is a different scale black whole – at this level everything is the same thing all wrapped up inside a single black whole fractal series! Or from a different perspective you could say everything is a fractal series of differnet scale singularities. Do you get the point? This is not the traditional black hole theory, but one that allows feedback via the opposite of a black hole, a white hole. The term whole is used in place of hole to represent the wholeness of a complete system - remember fundamentally everything is one.

Haramein's theory proposes the event (light) horizon of a black whole stores all the information of our 3D universe in 2 dimensions. Our universe is made up of self similar black wholes at different scales with all the information of all time stored at every point - just like a hologram stores all the information at every point within the hologram. For more in depth understanding, check out Nassim Haramein's paper on Quantum Gravity and the Holographic Mass.

Where are my binoculars?

From our perspective (biology), the largest thing known to man is the observable universe which spans approximately 93 billion light years and growing. The universe is believed to be expanding 'from our point of view' at an ever increasing rate, which means light (information) beyond this horizon does not have time to reach us, if such information exists. This establishes a boundary condition. This is an extremely important point as it has major implications for the foundations the Big Bang theory is built upon. Visualise what we are being told. The furthest galaxies, whose light signatures we can measure, are flying away from each other at increasingly faster speeds, which - by definition - must reach infinity. Also note: is it really galaxies we are measuring, or light itself - which we already know has infinite speed - at least from one perspective? Interestingly, we predict the diameter of the observable universe from a radius that we measure to be approximately 46 billion light years - which we can see from our perspective in all directions. This confirms we are at the centre of the universe, at least the observable one and with quantum physics slapping us around the face with a wet dishcloth screaming "you are the observer of your personal reality tunnel!!!" also adds credence to your role in the whole performance. It also supports the theory the universe itself appears to be spherical. More evidence for this is in the shape of the WMAP's early universe mapping the cosmic microwave background radiation which is a 2D picture of a 3D sphere.

Photo courtesy of NASA

On this note it is always about perspective whether something appears spherical or disc shaped in nature. Believe it or not the flat earth theory has attracted legions of believers in recent years backed up by compelling evidence. We assume the earth, other planetary bodies and stars to be spherical in shape yet larger galactic entities such as our solar system, galaxies and - from certain quarters it is believed the universe itself - are disc shaped. Add to that how our perceptions of the world we live on suggest it to be flat. Both theories are very difficult if not impossible to disprove fully. Think of it this way; your sensory perception would suggest you live on a relatively flat spinning disc, though from a higher vantage point a sphere seems more appropriate. Yet, when we observe further (galaxies) it changes back to the perception of a spinning disc. This is the duality of perspective and it's the paradox of the world we live in. It's my belief perspective allows every story to be told from the opposite viewpoint. But for the purpose of simplification I have chosen to tell it from the more commonly held belief of spheres. Interestingly the double torus geometry works from both perspectives.

The other big question in cosmology is "do we live in a finite universe or is the universe infinite?" For a number of weeks, just after I began writing this book, I had a nagging compulsion to do a simple calculation. I multiplied the speed of light in miles per second (186,200) by the number of seconds in a year (31,536,000) to obtain the number of miles light travels in one year (5.872e+12). Knowing that we have calculated the observable universe to have a radius of somewhere between 46 and 46.5 billion light years I discovered something quite fascinating. If we multiply (5.872e+12) by (46 billion) we get (2.7e+23). This I realised is a derivative of Euler's number, which is the exponential function. Euler's number to 6 decimal places is 2.718281, but continues to infinity with no repeating pattern and is at the base of the logarithmic scale. Like pi it is one of the few transcendental numbers and considered one of the most important numbers in all of mathematics. Consequently, by flipping the equation, if I multiply the speed of one light year (5.872e+12) by Euler's number to 10 decimal places (2.7182818284e+23) we can calculate a more accurate radius of the observable universe (46.2400928090 billion light years). With Euler's number being transcendental, which means of a spiritual non physical realm, it suggests the Universe is infinite. 'Seek and ye shall find' - the further or deeper we look, the more things we will see. The irony is, we as observers put it there, yet are blinded to this. It is our observations that create the Universe, but this is only half the story. To be continued......

Where's my magnifying glass?

From the largest to the smallest, lets delve a little deeper. The Planck scale, which is also referred to as the Zero point field or Vacuum density, is the source of all information. This field resides at absolute zero, permeates all of spacetime, and is created from nothing by 'virtual' particles of matter and antimatter colliding to release energy at the smallest scale measurable. As previously discussed these vacuum fluctuations are little spherical Planck length oscillators that overlap, in a flower of life pattern, producing a vibration and each one can be thought of as a single bit of information (a photon of light). Energy, information and light at source therefore would appear to be one and the same. The whole universe appears to us to be composed of light oscillating at different frequencies of charge, manifesting the matter of our perceptions through the 'formatting of action within', which is information. Action being angular momentum (spin). In other words if energy was not informed what to be or do, how could it transform into anything else? At the level of consciousness of biology the mind creates the separation of energy, information and light to produce the variety we experience in nature.

Einstein described gravity at the cosmological level as the surface of spacetime curving. Think of a stretched out bed sheet pulled tightly (spacetime) and let a ball rest at its centre (celestial object). The mass of the ball will warp the bed sheet around it. The greater the mass, the greater the curvature, the greater the gravitational pull. Please note, spacetime is 4 co-ordinates, this is nothing substantial. Therefore the fabric (bed sheet) that makes up Einstein's spacetime is only an analogy. It doesn't actually exist. It is light curving around what we perceive as an object but is really a perturbation within light itself - much the same as a whirlpool in the medium of water. A whirltpool is a body of swirling water produced by the meeting of opposing currents which creates a vortex. This is the same vorticular dynamics that exist within each Planck oscillation, every proton in the nucleus of an atom, every celestial body and black hole. Remember, light is the carrier of the electromagnetic charge, which manifests as a charged region of space (perturbation) from the angular momentum of the Planck oscillations into what we perceive as matter.

Now let's connect what Haramein is telling us is happening at the quantum level, the smallest perceived field. At this virtual level the universe is being created from energy in the form of little spherical photons or Planck scale units (PSU)s. When torque and the coriolis effect are added and by incorporating all the (PSU)s to Einstein's gravitational field equations, which form the basis for gravity in general relativity, Haramein was able to calculate the gravitational force at the quantum level. The torque and coriolis force create an effect similar to water going down a drain, which when incorporated into the dynamics of a black whole, instead of forming a perfect sphere create the topology of a double torus. This is two doughnut shaped structures one on top of the other, with a singularity at the centre, which rotates in opposite directions incorporating feedback. This suggests the whole universe is made of mini black wholes – a kind of multiverse. For this to be meaningful he needed to show how the connection to the world at the level of matter creation worked.

Rewind to 1917 when a New Zealand born British scientist, Ernest Rutherford, discovered the only seemingly solid part of an atom, the proton. He discovered the proton was the only part of the atom that caused a repelling effect due to its positive charge with the rest being empty space. Therefore solidity arises from an electrically charged region of space and must only be an illusion! The proton in the atoms nucleus was only 0.00001% of the atom. A century ago this was mind blowing. If you are only hearing this for the first time it should also be mind blowing because everything that your five senses perceive is 99.99999% empty space. Remember though, in the world of our perceptions nothing is 100%, everything is paradoxical. This is because the smaller we delve the more energy exists, but let's stick with the current paradigm's way of thinking. It is accepted as 'solid' science that the whole universe is made from atoms, hence 0.00001% can only be considered as solid. The 3% that we can see is the light emitted from galaxies and stars. But remember, light is massless, so the question is: how is something so tiny as the proton generating the matter of our perceptions?

Before we go there, I think I need to set the scene with the current model in physics which predicts four fundamental universal forces. It's from these force fields that particles manifest into our everyday reality. The macro-verse of electromagnetism and gravity is the atomic level, whilst the micro-verse of the strong and its corresponding weak nuclear force (which hold the atomic nucleus in place) is the sub-atomic realm. The boundary condition is at the level of the atom with, two forces on the outside and two on the inside - one expansive and one contractive on each side of the boundary. In essence this is the boundary condition of biology; homeostasis intact. So far so good, except this is not the fundamental level of matter creation; the universal pattern never begins with four of anything.

There are two major fundamental boundary conditions that exist from your point of view. The boundary between spirit and the mind/body and the boundary between mind and body (the sub-atomic realm of energy/information linked to your thoughts and feelings and the atomic realm of what you perceive to experience). At each boundary condition the law of opposites applies and when we fully embrace this we will see the pattern to how everything functions and comes into being.

From the spiritual perspective everything is connected, everything is one - yet spirit is 'potentially' nothing or no-thing. Therefore crossing the first boundary condition nothing must become something and simultaneously become everything. On the other side of the boundary we have the mind, so with spirit being 'one' whole, the mind must be 'dual' in nature, thus we have mind and body. You see, the term 'body' is referencing the material world we experience. It is actually an 'immaterial' mental world, created through the mind, yet experienced as a solid 'material' reality. This tangible world of objects (electromagnetism), having crossed the boundary, stems from an intangible, subjective observer. This subjective duality of thoughts and feelings is imprinted into the system (gravity) and is what we feed back to spirit as an experience. Notice the pattern - one becomes two (spirit becomes the duality of mind) whilst simultaneously the one mind is infinite (mind becomes the infinite world of experience). It is the paradox of how the one becomes the many and the many are the one, dependent on the perspective taken in all its myriad of guises.

With the solid world really being a mental shadow it fits perfectly with the holographic principle. When we peer deeper into reality we see the fractal nature unveil itself. Scientists were astonished to discover that what appeared as a substantial material world to our senses, when viewed under a microscope, faded into insubstantial probability waves of potential, right before their eyes. Isn't it ironic the greatest vanishing act in the history of the universe is the universe itself!

Now is the time (now there's a paradox) to bring consciousness (or what we have referenced as spirit) into the equation as the ground state of being. Looking from the opposite perspective of biology nothing exists but potentials and for this nothingness to become something a boundary condition must be crossed. It becomes something from our perspective at the level of the positively electrically charged proton. Our sensory apparatus for seeing, hearing, touching, tasting and smelling is all based on our perceptions of energy vibrating at differing frequencies. Did you know that we never touch anything? Nothing does!

What we sense is the positively charged protons in say our fingers coming into close proximity with the positively charged protons of the object in question. This is due to the repelling effect of two positive charges. What we are really touching is the space in between which we have previously mentioned to be the connector of all things. This 'illusory space' is how energy/information is exchanged in both directions, between the consciousness at the level of spirit and the same consciousness at the level of biology.

> "Biology is the feedback mechanism for
> the universe to learn more about itself"
>
> - Nassim Haramein

Einstein's most famous equation $E=MC^2$ tells us everything in the universe is energy. Energy in its purest state is undefinable. 'Change' from one instant to the next defines what energy does, but that's not what energy is. In actual fact what is being measured is the 'potential' difference from one moment or 'still' frame to another moment or 'still' frame. Can you see the connection to spirituality? The measurement of energy (scientific model) involves the potential change in stillness (spiritual model) from the point of view of the observer.

The initial boundary condition exists at the Planck scale. This scale is outside of our sensory awareness, but would appear to be the origin of energy, information and light. It's from this wholly trinity that consciousness manifests the atomic level of matter with which our senses interact.

The multiverse

By calculating the ratio between the number of Planck scale fluctuations in the volume of a proton and its surface area, Haramein was able to predict not only the proton's mass, but also the charge radius of the proton, within a margin of error, to experimental evidence to a much greater accuracy than the standard model. He was then able to calculate, with the addition of spin, the gravity of such an object and it gave the exact range we measure the strong force to be, between two protons in the nuclei of an atom. The inevitable conclusion is that the strong force is gravity in the quantum domain, due to the interaction of the Planck scale vacuum fluctuations.

With Haramein also able to predict the mass of the proton, something else extraordinary came to light. Using classical mechanics instead of quantum theory Haramein discovered the proton to be much heavier than the standard models proton. In fact, the energy calculated was the same as the mass of the entire universe. Hang about! I hear you cry. How can something billions of times smaller than a grain of sand contain the same amount of energy as the whole universe? Therein lies the paradox. Space from our human perspective is the connector of all things. So is space the answer? Well, yes and no. Within the physics model the answer is yes, but we know models are a sub-set of who is asking the question. So who is it that is asking the question? You are! You are the boundary condition between the outer universal world and the inner quantum world, and it's from this point of view that space is the connector of all things, with this based on the principle of the law of opposites.

Having established that it is biology that is central (perfect equilibrium) to the outer and inner worlds, it is easier to accept that the further we observe in either direction the greater the energy. Biology creates its own boundaries, the outer boundary of the observable universe having a mass of 10^{55} grams and the inner boundary, at the level of the proton, with each proton having the same energy 10^{55} grams. This is the fundamental fractal nature of you. Once again, it's the paradox of the one and the many, with consciousness writing the script.

A basic law in physics is that energy cannot be created or destroyed, it always transforms. This must then apply to information. As previously mentioned, they are both manifestations of the same thing. This being the case, then all of the information of the universe is present inside the volume of a proton. Evidence suggests protons act like tiny worm holes, which are all entangled, feeding off the vacuum density fluctuations. This fits with the holographic model. Every point in space holds all of the information. The proton is essentially a collection of Planck scale electromagnetic charge fluctuations spinning in an area of space which we identify as a particle. This is not our standard worldview of solidity. Solidity it appears, is a form of electromagnetically charged particles vibrating at different frequencies. It is all a matter of perspective, with the tiny humble proton being the level of matter creation. Enter the multiverse. If every proton contains all the energy and information of the universe then it doesn't require a quantum leap to accept that every proton is a universe in and of itself. From your point of view, you create a single reality tunnel which you perceive as the universe, all created from a multiverse of protons within this universe. We have been told through the ages by the spiritual masters to look within for the answers!

> "What we call matter is really just specific dynamics of the field we are bathing in."

> -Nassim Haramein

In Haramein's paper the Schwarzschild proton, for which he won a coveted physics award, he shows mathematically the organised scaling laws of the entire universe - from the Planck scale all the way up to universal level - with biology turning up dead centre. This is mathematical proof of what spirituality has been telling us for eons. Add to that the recent discovery of the cosmic (light) horizon, extending equally in all directions, and that also confirms that you are the centre of the universe. It predicts that everything exhibits holographic black hole dynamics in an infinitely repeating pattern. So you can now think of the dynamics of a black hole as creative rather than destructive. Or as Haramein puts it, a black whole, which also contains a white hole to allow for expansion and contraction, fitting nicely with the double torus topology. The way it appears depends on where you are in relation to the event horizon. On the outside, the black whole will appear very bright, like those we observe at the centre of galaxies. However, if you are on the inside of a black whole it will appear dark, just like the night sky. Yes it would seem we live inside a black whole and, due to fractality, other black wholes are observable from this vantage point. If you remember, in chapter 2, I had come to the same conclusion, using the feedback loop of the law of opposites. Haramein has produced mathematical proof to confirm this.

Another paradox we experience is the emptiness of space. As mentioned in chapter 1 the vacuum density is many orders of magnitude greater than the entire mass of the universe, and it would therefore appear infinitely dense. Yet our sensory awareness perceives it as empty. Haramein theorises this is because the structure of space itself is in a state of perfect equilibrium. I believe the state of perfect equilibrium is the still point at the centre of the law of opposites feedback loop. This would tie in with our emotional state. When we are relaxed everything feels centred, but a slight emotional deviation can either make things feel heavier when tense or lighter when we are elated.

The way I see it, the standard model in cosmology needs a number of little tweaks, two major role reversals and one helluva kick up its dogmatic backside! A lot of blood, sweat and tears in the science community over hundreds of years has given us so much, but yet the holy grail in physics - the unified theory of everything - appears as far away as ever. String theorists, with their ten plus dimensions, have tied themselves in mathematical knots. General relativity, as it's commonly taught, totally unravels within the black holes it first predicted. Through renormalisation processes quantum theory has managed to be twisted inside out. Mind blowing at the very least!

For the theory of everything, or at least an awareness of the pattern and dynamics of potentially everything, the modern scientific method requires a healthy dose of spiritual open mindedness. A merging of eastern and western thought and emotion, plus inner awareness and outer experience, are needed to unite as one. You cannot omit no-thing if your goal is to unite everything.

To be or not to be

The holy grail in physics is to unite the four fundamental forces, and, if you were to unite them in such a way that all were one, well.....I think this would not only put the icing on the cake, but the cherry on the top too. The first chapter in this book talked about life being paradoxical. The second showed how the paradox comes about, through the law of opposites feedback loop, based on the power of three. This is where science and spirituality merge. In spirituality we have previously concluded there are two boundary conditions. We can also think of these boundary conditions as mirror reflections. The world we live in appears localised and, for the most part, linear time based in nature, although expressed paradoxically from non local fields. Non locality is dimensionless, there is no first or second, but our minds function sequentially so for simplicity we will say the initial mirror boundary condition arises between spirit/ consciousness and the mind. A boundary condition is like looking into a mirror and seeing an opposite reflection. In other words when a boundary condition is crossed the opposite of itself manifests. This initial boundary crossing creates duality. Think of it this way. Stand in front of a mirror and observe yourself. There now appears two of you. You and your mirror image only flipped. If a second mirror is introduced behind where you're standing you will now observe an infinity of versions of self. For infinity to occur a second boundary condition must be crossed. This is the world you embody, not only your experience of reality, but also the vessel you inhabit to experience reality with. This world that manifests on the outside, including your body vessel, is an infinite expression of spirit/consciousness, but functions in an opposite manner to your inner world of thoughts and feelings.

We're almost virtually there!

To recap: in the standard model of physics the outer world comprises two fundamental forces; electromagnetism (expansion) and gravity (contraction). The inner quantum world of sub-atomic particles also has two fundamental forces; the strong nuclear force (contraction) and weak nuclear force (expansion). For the standard models theory to work it requires all four of the fundamental forces to involve the exchange of force carrier particles. They are the photon (electromagnetism), the graviton (gravity), the gluon (strong force) and W and Z bosons (weak force). The exchanges are either attractive or repulsive. These so called particles are created and exist only in the exchange process, and they are therefore known within the model as virtual particles. Let me repeat that…….they are considered virtual particles. What this means is they never actually exist in space and time. I find it hard to accept that the standard model can label something a particle that never actually forms. On top of all that, the graviton has never been detected. Therefore, their theoretical mathematical model is incomplete.

Also, the strong nuclear force was given its name due to the theory that something must exist to hold the protons so tightly together that it will keep them from repelling each other in such a small space as the nucleus of an atom. Due to the massive amount of energy contained within the proton, the repulsive positive charge forces required an astronomically strong force to hold it together, hence the name the strong force. Ironically due to the existence of the strong force a corresponding weak nuclear force was also calculated to exist. The weak nuclear force is crucial to the structure of the universe. It is a radioactive force that decays with its exchange particles being the 'massive' W and Z boson. I must stress both of these forces were calculated due to the initial assumption made by the standard model. The assumption being that the world we live in is material, therefore composed of solid particles. This I have shown time and again throughout the book, from many different view points, is not the case. I have even highlighted the standard models own paradoxical assumptions.

We know from the holographic perspective the strong force is not required. It is gravity on the inside of the boundary condition. This also does away with the need for the graviton which has never been found to exist anyway. Logically our next step is to see if there is a connection between the electromagnetic force......and the inner electroweak force. As their names suggest, a link does exist. The electroweak and electromagnetic forces are linked through what is known as electroweak unification and fundamentally, when the universe was extremely hot, they could be thought of as one and the same force. With the present relatively low universal temperatures, these fundamental forces appear very different - the exchange particle of electromagnetism (photon) being massless and the exchange particles for the electroweak interaction being massive. This has been labelled spontaneous symmetry breaking and therefore the two forces are thought of as separate. The key to all this is the assumption that if the electroweak and electromagnetic forces are essentially the same, then they must also have the same strength. I will challenge this assumption shortly. The standard model does say that, at extremely high temperatures unification with the strong force and gravity is achievable, with the four fundamental forces all being a single unified force. This is known as grand unification.

It would appear grand unification is within touching distance, but only if we include Haramein's quantum gravity and the holographic mass theory which mathematically shows gravity and the strong force are one and the same. The graviton can remain buried in the rabbit hole as its not required. On top of all this Haramein's theory does away with the need for dark matter and dark energy - the 97% of the universe which is undetectable in the standard model. It is the vacuum density's contractive and repulsive electromagnetic structure of space itself that holds galaxies together and, at the same time, pushes them apart at ever increasing rates. At the time of writing, the Laser interferometer Gravitational Wave Observatory (LIGO) has just announced the first confirmation of the detection of gravitational waves, predicted by Einstein many decades previous. A report in New Scientist magazine a few weeks later put forward the supposition "did LIGO detect dark matter?" The article advised "Dark matter might be made of black holes and gravitational waves could help us find out." It went on to say "if these black holes exist today in great enough numbers, they could make up dark matter, the mysterious substance that comprises 85% of the universe's mass yet gives no sign of its presence except through gravity." It then says "but so far there is no firm evidence for their existence." Anyone interested read the papers on Quantum Gravity and the Holographic Mass by Nassim Haramein and you just might disagree.

Having realised quantum gravity, the standard models strong force, and universal gravity are manifestations of the same force, I looked into how they are connected. If we apply the law of opposites feedback loop, with you being the boundary condition, what we would expect to find is the gravitational force to be very weak on one side and incredibly strong on the other, and that's exactly what we get. Gravity at the universal level is considered the weakest of the standard model's four forces whilst quantum gravity is calculated to be extremely strong. Another thing I haven't mentioned, that fits the law of opposites principle, is the range of forces with universal gravity stretched across all of space, and quantum gravity being limited within the nucleus of an atom.

Presently we have three forces; electromagnetism on the outside of the boundary with the weak force on the inside, and gravity, which is perpetually exchanging information with the vacuum either side of the boundary - but here is the key, it's manifesting in an opposite fashion. The next challenge was to see if electromagnetism and the weak force can be united as one and the same using the law of opposites principle. As I discovered, electromagnetism and the weak force are connected as the same force at higher temperatures, but spontaneously break apart at lower temperatures. Both forces radiate and decay to form new elements which are responsible for the variety of our objective experiences. Let's apply the law of opposites. The exchange particle of electromagnetism is the photon which is massless with infinite range. The W and Z bosons are considered massive with a calculated range of 0.1% of the diameter of a proton. This range is unimaginably minuscule! So far the principle is right on the money. The question now is, can the law of opposites resolve the spontaneous symmetry breaking problem? Yes! The law of opposites states that, from the current boundary condition point of view, the assumption that electromagnetism and the weak force should have the same strength is incorrect. The strengths should manifest as the opposite to each other and that is exactly the case! What we can conclude is that the weak nuclear force is the manifestation of the electromagnetic force at the atomic level. Now we have two – electromagnetism and gravity. On top of that there is only a requirement for one 'virtual' exchange particle - the photon. Remember, it's at the vacuum density, where the photons originate as the Planck scale units that emit light and at the same time feedback the information via their vorticular dynamics.

It is believed grand unification requires only one force, but that only holds true from the spiritual perspective. From the perspective of biology (you) the one force will appear to have two opposing sides, but is really entangled as one. One of the fundamental laws in physics tells us that for every action there is an equal and opposite reaction. Every expansion requires a contraction and every contraction requires an expansion. The expansive electromagnetic force and the contractive gravity are inextricably linked as one. They are two sides of the same coin. Gravity is electromagnetism in reverse. Ironically, the standard model is in agreement with this, as it predicts when the early universe (in the beginning) was extremely hot there was only one force – Electromagnetism.

In the beginning was the word and that word was a hum!

CHAPTER 6

Follow the Money

Why is the world the way it is? It is this way by design. For most their personal lives are quite humdrum. "Same old same old" is a common synopsis offered when asked "what's new?". Day to day living can be very mundane and repetitive. It helps us define who we think we are. We could refer to it as small picture syndrome. Then, punctured throughout the day we are reminded of the bigger picture, which quite often is nuts! We have, for example, earthquakes, tsunami's, wars, beheadings, banking collapses, world poverty, dictatorships, more taxes, sporting achievements, human endeavour and the occasional cat stuck up a tree. This system of bombardment of local and world news is just another example of the law of opposites in play; the human and humanity. As we know, the law of opposites requires a process and that's what this chapter is focused on.

The need to spend

"Money is the root of all evil". I'm sure we have all heard the phrase, but money in and of itself is just a symbol; it's a collective agreement that something of no tangible value is valuable. I think a more accurate claim would be "the love of money is the root of all evil". You see, money can be likened to energy. The more money you have the more energy you have. The more energy you have the more you can do. To do is to take action and to take action is to create. Money does not increase your creative ability, that power is unlimited when you allow yourself to remove all of your self imposed boundaries, but it does assist greatly in the belief of doing so.

For money to have value, society must form an agreement. Herein lies the fractal pattern of money. We begin with individuals who come together to form a collective: a society. The next fractal leap is when individual societies come together to form a co-operative, examples being the European Union and the United States of America. This fractal monetary system has evolved to humanity itself where countries trade with different currencies and have formed agreements and how each relates to their value. At every level the system evolves into greater complexity, but always through the original basic principles.

"The quest for certainty in a world of uncertainty creates some amusing parallels between the life of an individual and that of society"

-Robert Anton Wilson

Relax – no thinking required

Society, as a functioning entity, has no conscience - in a sense it is robotic in nature. How many laws are we subjected to that seem ludicrous? Conscience resides within the individual not the collective. The individual cannot be completely free within a society. You are always bound by the societal constraints. Herein lies the paradox: the one (free spirit) and the many (society). If you want to function in society you must be prepared to give up some of your power, but hopefully not too much. Do you want to become a pawn and blindly allow yourself to be controlled and manipulated in such a way as to be put in the position to cause loss or harm to another or yourself. Enter the Military.

'All hail our heroes' is the latest propaganda we are subjected to. Men and women who fight for their country, go off to far away lands in the name of peace, but unfortunately still are ordered to kill and maim anyone who stands in their way. The soldier mentality is to operate from 'the facts' typically knowing the 'what' of the matter, but most often not being privy to the 'why' or 'how'. They are told to do, not asked. A soldier is generally pigeon holed; not being made aware of the bigger picture (which helps to nullify conscience) executing his orders without question - even to the point of killing another person. They are trained to believe it's for the greater good – that the rest of the world benefits. Then we wonder why so many come back from the battlefield traumatised and unable to function in civvy street.

Innocent until proven guilty I believe.......maybe not anymore. Just like in the Tom Cruise movie Minority Report, where future events were foreseen by gifted humans known as Pre-Cogs to prevent a crime before it took place, the powers that be choose to invade other countries to seek out and destroy in an attempt to prevent another 9/11 or 7/7 or Madrid bombing or Paris attack.......the list goes on. I am not a complete pacifist. I believe there is an argument for an army to have the right to defend its own, but as soon as it becomes the aggressor you will find resistance always meets resistance. Is there any country in the world that will invite an invader in? There will always be a section, but I've still to hear of a democratic vote within the country taking place, to invoke such an invasion. Just contemplate on all the families that have been torn apart through such acts. Ask yourself, if you were in that position would it be worth potentially losing your children and loved ones? Which is more important, a country or your family? Life always provides another option. Human rights is generally rolled out to justify overthrowing a government, but who is it that is making this decision and why? Could there be a hidden agenda? Propaganda is widespread throughout most countries. The media is heavily censored and in the west journalists have morphed into reporters. A journalist would typically dig deep into events, to uncover unknowns, and to seek a balanced view, whereas a reporter provides us with the 'propaganated' (my term) facts. The United Nations were formed shortly after The Second World War, in place of the ineffective League of Nations, in an attempt to prevent the occurrence of a Third World War. From the outside it would appear to have certain rules for some countries and different rules for others. Currently they do not appear to be doing a particularly good job.

> "Those who are able to see beyond the shadows and lies of their culture will never be understood, let alone believed by the masses".

> -Plato

The spirit level is the key

Western society goes to war in the name of freedom. Freedom from what? Oppression? Oppression from who? Eastern society? And vice versa. Both societies are required to balance each other. Take one away and the other loses its identity. This balance centres around the Middle East where East meets West. For the world to be at peace requires this region to be stable. The question then arises: Why upset the whole apple cart, immediately after the Second World War, by the creation of The State of Israel? In doing so, whatever status quo existed beforehand is well and truly screwed now! Let me state that I have no gripe with any individuals, no matter their religion, race or creed. My belief is we are all one, no one being any better than anyone else. There is no room for a chosen race. I do know that as soon as labels and judgements are made conflict is just around the corner. Isn't it just as well we do not have a four way split with the inclusion of northern society and southern society. This just doesn't happen, as I've shown in the previous chapter, in connection with the universal forces. Life manifests as opposites, embedded or layered within other opposites, with the middle ground in between the polar divisions maintaining the balance. In Buddhism we are ushered towards the middle path where balance lies. This is THE SYSTEM. Lets look at the system from another angle.

If it doesn't feel right it probably isn't

Currently the education system in the western world churns out intelligently suppressed brainwashed people all of the time. The ones that do well at school tend to be those who can download and regurgitate information most effectively. The education system over recent decades has been blatantly dumbed down. We are generally taught through repetition. Like everything in life there are always benefits to this process, but it doesn't allow much scope for personal creativity or reward. If you don't follow the methodology, and come up with the preordained answer, you don't get rewarded with the marks - irrespective of your final outcome. The system operated in this way produces a great deal of intelligent zombies; people who are prepared to work within the system, regardless of whether it appears right or wrong to them. Stick within the rules and a good job, that pays well, is waiting for you at the end. On the surface you might ask "What is wrong with that?" I've proved my ability to perform at a level required for my chosen profession. The problem with this system is the same as every controlled system.......the established order. For the established order - more commonly referred to as The Establishment - to exist, a system to control the masses must be put in place. If we don't have order we have chaos, but we fail to recognise that too much of anything is NOT a good thing. Keep people on the straight and narrow and they will act as puppets, looking in the same place, hoping to find something new but only reinforcing the old guard. Let's keep building larger and more expensive particle colliders to smash particles together at ever increasing speeds, only to find smaller and smaller particles every time, but never anything fundamental. Keep doing what you're doing and you'll keep getting what you're getting springs to mind.

If it's broken.........fix it!

According to the biologist, Bruce Lipton PhD, the central dogma in mainstream science can be traced back to 1953, when Watson and Crick discovered DNA. Deoxyribonucleic acid - to give it its full title - is the genetic blueprint of information storage for all biology. Genes and the genome are made of DNA with a gene consisting of enough DNA to code for one protein whilst the genome is simply the sum total of an organism's DNA. Proteins are what generate movement in the body via electromagnetic charge but it was the Darwinian notion, in The Origin of Species, which appears to have led to the belief that genes control biology. The central dogma - as it's become known - is based upon the primacy of DNA. In simple terms it states that when a protein breaks down a xerox copy of the protein, ribonucleic acid (RNA), is produced from DNA to repair it - proteins being the body's building blocks. This allows biology to repair itself from damage and, for a time, ageing. This system of biological information flow is to this day believed by many to operate in only one direction; DNA to RNA to protein, with absolutely no feedback. This would suggest that we are genetically programmed from birth (a victim of our hereditary genes) and there's not a whole lot we can do about it. The pharmaceutical industry jumped right on board, advising us the only way to go was to pop pills to mask symptoms or, in more severe cases, inject poisonous substances destroying unhealthy as well as healthy cells - or better still, get butchered! Ok, maybe a little dramatic, and to be fair there are times, especially with today's conditioning, when surgery to remove parts of the body is the best way to go under the circumstances. However, this sadly is 21st century medical procedure and it's all pretty much based upon the outdated notion of the primacy of DNA.

A decade or two later came the discovery of epigenetics. This would turn the whole thing upside down literally. 'Epi' is derived from Greek to mean 'above' or 'before'. In essence every gene has a switch which can be turned on or off and, when on, can be upregulated or downregulated. It has been discovered that it's your perception of the environment that impacts your gene expression. A simple example would be: when you find something genuinely funny, your gene expression works in accordance by switching hundreds of genes on and others off, to allow for the release of the feel good hormones serotonin and dopamine which, in turn, provides for a healthier bodily expression. Likewise, the opposite happens when you're stressed. I don't think it's any great leap to suggest that those who worry lots tend to suffer greater ill health than those who offer a more prolonged happier disposition. For evolution to occur in any system it must allow for feedback to take place, otherwise no change occurs, leading inevitably to systematic death. All closed loop systems break down and eventually die.

With the new science of epigenetics came the discovery of the feedback of information from the proteins and RNA. As we now know, the feedback loop is essential to allow for open loop evolution. The realisation that it is an environmental signal, that activates the gene code via regulatory proteins to produce RNA, also destroyed the myth that we are a victim of our genes. The new science is called the primacy of the environment. You might have heard the term 'you are a product of your environment' but this is not wholly correct. To be more accurate you are a product of the meaning you put to your environment. The revised order of information flow is as follows: environmental signal to regulatory proteins to DNA to RNA to protein, and then information is fed back from the protein to RNA to DNA to regulatory proteins to environmental signal. The reverse flow of information is restricted somewhat to prevent radical changes to DNA.

This sounds wonderful. Victims no more. We are empowered. We take back the reigns of our own destiny......or do we? You see, even though the new science emerged, it is rarely taught to our medical students, who still believe in the old paradigm - but why? You do not have to look any further than vested interests!

The corporate psychopath

Doctors perform wonderful feats of achievement everyday, but I feel have to do so with their hands tied behind their backs, dangling upside down from the rafters. Seven years of medical school brainwashing, memorising exceedingly long strung out words with lots of x's and y's in them. This all spawns from the pharmaceutical industry, whose web of control, at every level, infiltrates the medical system like a virus. 'Big Pharma' as it is now known subsidises the medical students through university. It pays for medical schools, aids universities and funds medical research in disease and illness (which is also highly subsidised by a proliferation of well meaning charities). At the same time convincing the students throughout their medical training that synthetic drugs are the only way, by setting the course agendas, and then lobbying the same people, when qualified, to promote and hand out their drugs at a very hefty profit. This is a well oiled, well established, corporate idealistic system. I use the term idealistic in referencing its belief in perfection. Unfortunately this perfection hasn't much to do with healing, but more to do with profit. A large part of the western medical industry is based around illness and disease management as opposed to tangible health care. A sick population will always be much more profitable than a healthy one, at least from the industries point of view.

Ask yourself this question, why would any business resolve a problem which would in effect potentially put them out of business, or at the very least cause a severe dent in their profits? Think THE CANCER INDUSTRY!

Statistically, in the 1950's, in the west, the likelihood of being diagnosed with cancer was one in ten. This rose to one in three in the 1990's, with murmurings that it is close to a one in two ratio at the time of writing. We are told this is because we are living longer, so if this is the case, why do we continually raise so much money to give to the pharmaceutical industry, to keep doing the same things (with very little end product)? Ok, every so often we hear, via the heavily censored news, that there has been a breakthrough in the war against cancer. A seven year clinical trial will then begin, and - if successful - the product might then be available to the public (if there are public funds available or your medical insurance cover is sufficient). There are the aforementioned educated people, who will inform us that statistics prove that - in certain areas - success has been achieved and, to be fair, on the surface this would appear to be the case. But this should not mask the inadequacies of the current system. The war on cancer has had so much money 'apparently' thrown at it, and yet it is still one of the most feared words in society. Something has to give!

> "Insanity is doing the same things over and over again expecting different results"
>
> -pretty much all of us

Before I move on I would like to take this opportunity to show how the cancer industry, which also includes a lot of the related charities, knowingly or unknowingly perpetuate the fear into the psyche of contracting cancer. In Northern Ireland alone we have Cancer Focus, Cancer Awareness, Action Cancer, Cancer Research, Breast Cancer Awareness, Prostate Cancer Awareness and the list goes on. In psychology it is well documented the subconscious mind records and downloads all information, most often storing at a deeper level, which can impact you dramatically without you being consciously aware. Whatever you focus your attention on, you energise. When you're constantly made aware of something, your attention will always be drawn to that something. What impact do you think the words Cancer 'Awareness' have, on top of all the other times cancer is mentioned in the media? You can imagine it would make you very much aware of the potential for you to get cancer, especially if it's something that you worry about and fear.

Expand your beliefs

The mind subjectively puts meaning to objectively boxed people, places, circumstances and events that it creates in the first place. From this, each one of us assembles a belief system that becomes our worldview. This worldview is highly impacted by your environmental upbringing which includes your peers. The influence of peers creates agreements of consensual reality which is just a larger box. I guess your definitions of the world could be thought of as a fractal of boxes; boxes or boundaries embedded within one another.

Anybody who attempts to think and voice an opinion outside the box is quite often labelled a quack or quirky at best. Most of us operate within the box and tend to agree with what the mainstream psyche perpetuates through education and the media. To constantly question is seen as conspiratorial and odd - maybe even having delusions of grandeur. To remain within the box can feel comfortable by accepting the general opinion - and when the general opinion is inconclusive, then just ignore until the general opinion evolves to a level that you blindly accept once more. Remember, a problem cannot be resolved at the level it was created, therefore to resolve anything we must be able to observe the bigger picture, which requires us to step outside the box. This then sets you apart from the herd mentality, and unfortunately, due to the strength of people's belief in their personal worldview, can appear to them as antagonistic. Problem is, if no one ever offered an opinion outside of the general consensus the world would be stuck in a status quo never to evolve.

Your life arises from your own point of view. The holofractographic model and spirituality are in complete agreement that the power always (from every point) resides in you. Therefore, if general opinion is saying you have a 50/50 chance of getting cancer, then step outside the box and ask yourself the relevant questions. Allow the answers to your questions to flow naturally - and they will - and then integrate a more empowering belief into your worldview. In the words of Rocky Balboa "that's how winning is done".

Cheque the foundations

At the beginning of this chapter we talked about what money is. Let me conclude with how money is created - with a very brief synopsis of the world banking system. After the latest world banking collapse in 2008, the 99% (as we are now known) had access to vast amounts of information relating to the history of banking with more and more of us becoming aware of how corrupt the banking system actually is.

At the core of this system is the role the central bank plays within almost every major country. It beggars belief that in a lot of cases the countries central banks act outside of the countries jurisdiction. For example there is nothing federal about the Federal Reserve in America. Its headquarters are in Washington D.C. which paradoxically is the capital of the United States yet is not within the United States. It functions and is governed in the same way the City of London operates outside of the United Kingdom – ironically where the Bank of England is located. The whole banking system is built upon smoke and mirrors!

The elected government of practically every democratic country in the world must go cap in hand to borrow money in the form of a LOAN from its central bank - which attaches interest to the loan. The central bank only manufactures the amount of the original loan, but never the interest accrued. The loan is deposited into a central bank account from which the money is distributed throughout the commercial banking chain. With every bank in the chain only required to hold around 10% in reserve of what is deposited, it allows the commercial banks to loan the other 90% which additionally has never been manufactured. This is known as fractional reserve lending and when you extrapolate this down the banking chain a huge amount of debt is created within the whole global monetary system. This system allows money to be created out of thin air much like Charlie the counterfeiter! It has been estimated that only 3% of physical money actually exists in the system – now where have we come across that figure before? Fractional reserve banking is the ultimate Ponzi scheme which interestingly is not taught in economics class.

According to some sources in 2015 the world debt figure stood at 60 trillion dollars. Would it surprise you to know that every country operates in debt. It acts as a form of debt slavery - but in debt to who? I don't think I need to tell you. The next question that springs to mind is why?

> "Permit me to issue and control the money of a nation, and I care not who makes the laws"

The above quote has been attributed to Mayer Amschel Rothschild (international banker), but is hard to prove. It matters not who originally said it - common sense suggests it would appear correct. It would seem on the surface the money lenders, pulling the strings behind the 'established' veil, are the worlds puppeteers!

In one respect this appears to be the case, but from another it most certainly is not! The purpose of this chapter was to provide a few examples as to why the outside world appears so chaotic at times, and acts as a veil, to hide and distract us from who is the real orchestrator!

CHAPTER 7

The Spiritual Perspective

For those not spiritually aware, do you think it might be time for you to let go of separation and victimisation, and take back responsibility to allow for the reconnection with your true self?

There are two main threads that run throughout this book. The catalyst was to extract clarity from the jumbled mess of thoughts running through my head and join the dots in a more coherent fashion, by putting down on print what I had become aware of on my journey of enlightenment. I will say again that I believe enlightenment is the journey, not the destination and all of us are at different points along this path. The second thread is to promote how the lesser known spiritual law of opposites, affects us all, on a moment to moment basis, and seems to be the answer to all of life's paradoxes. During the course of writing the book my eyes have been opened even more to the prevalence of this spiritual law, even to the point of the law of opposites itself having an opposite.........the more widely known law of attraction (like attracts like).

Spirituality is based on oneness centred around the concept of wholeness. Everything is imbued with spiritual conscious awareness. Linguistics is a model embedded within spiritual reality, so can never do it justice. In fact, all things connected to the mental and physical realms are models of reality, not reality itself. Reality itself is unknowable as our thoughts are also an activity within reality. Therefore reality cannot be fully comprehended by the mind. Having said all that, you are still aware a problem exists. Likewise, whatever reality is, it is aware of itself through you. Human beings possess this same self-awareness. This, I believe, is what is referred to in the bible as the image and likeness message. We are not a physical reflection, we are a reflection in consciousness. Fundamentally, reality is based in the absolute realm, whereas the mental and physical realms are relative and can be thought of as unfolding with the power of - and within - this absolute realm. Relative and absolute are opposites, one knowable - the other not. One is of dual nature and the other is singular. Amazingly, light, electricity, magnetism and energy are all absolute in nature. It is only in the realm of the relative that we can measure what they do, yet this does not tell us what they are. They would appear to be all one and the same potential.......therefore, unknowable. The formless becoming form.

David Bohm a protégé of Einstein referred to it as the implicate and explicate order. In his book, Wholeness and the Implicate Order, he coined the terms to describe two different frameworks for understanding the same phenomenon or aspect of reality. He developed a mathematical formula to describe the bizarre behaviour of sub-atomic particles at the quantum level, in respect to our physical experience of the world. He collaborated with Karl Pribram on how the brain appears to function like a hologram, in accordance with quantum mathematical principles, with the characteristics of wave patterns. They referred to it as the holonomic model.

"In the enfolded (or implicate) order, space and time are no longer the dominant factors determining the relationships of dependence or independence of different elements. Rather an entirely different sort of basic connection of elements is possible, from which our ordinary notions of space and time, along with those of separately existent material particles, are abstracted as forms derived from a deeper order. These ordinary notions in fact appear in what is called the explicate or "unfolded" order, which is a special and distinguished form contained within the general totality of all the implicate orders."

-David Bohm

The reality tunnels we construct mentally unfold whilst simultaneously curving back in on themselves in what appears from our perspective as a linear sequence of events but fundamentally it takes place in a single eternal moment.

An old zen proverb goes something like this – two monks discussing a flag blowing in the wind. One says it is only the flag that is moving whereas the other disagrees and claims it is only the wind that is moving. To settle their disagreement they approach the spiritual master and ask "master is it the flag moving in the wind or is it the wind moving the flag? The spiritual master with a forlorn look on his face tells them to wise up and do something useful!.......but then with a nondescript look informs them neither is correct – it is only consciousness that moves.

The manifestation perspective

From the human perspective we continually make the mistake that models of reality are reality itself. We all have the divine ability to create our own model of reality, due to each of us being an activity, not the whole, but all imbued with the power of the whole. Think of it this way. Every one of us being a dot, all joined as one whole, and, from this paradoxically undivided individuation we have a 'point' of view; a perspective that can reflect back on the whole, whilst containing or having access to all the information of the whole. In every moment, or the one eternal moment, points of view come into contact with other points of view, creating an interference pattern - and when the interference pattern is enlightened, reality tunnels are created, each appearing separate yet always connected. This is also the principle of a hologram. This paradoxically allows for free will in a deterministic environment, answering the age old question: Do we have free will, or is our fate predetermined? In our personal reality tunnel it is both - it's you who decides. You are the co-creator of your reality tunnel, along with the whole ensemble, and when you are able to come to terms with this it is up to you to take the reins of responsibility and let go of any victim complex.

> "If you think you can or you think you can't, you're right"
>
> -Henry Ford

Its all about perspective

The teachings of Jesus instruct us to love God and love thy neighbour as thyself. Spiritually this can be interpreted as 'love is'. You are God embodied, as is everyone and everything else. In other words, do not judge or label, in the belief that it is separate from you. To define is to label, but do so in the knowledge that your definition is only appearing as a different manifestation of the 'you' who is defining. Definitions are for embodied experiences. So choose wisely!

The teachings of Einstein promote that matter, energy, space and time are all the same thing, manifesting in different forms, to provide you with a playground to experience who you really are, from a unique point of view. It is so effective that you, for the most part, don't even realise you're doing it. This God fella is very clever! Undoubtedly the universal hide and seek champion. But getting back to Einstein, we can break it down more superficially into experiencing objective moving frames of reference. This creates the false belief that an objective world actually exists, outside of our subjective selves, to manufacture a belief that we are not worthy of the lofty heights of godliness.

Is the law of opposites at play here? Of course it is! One view claims I'm not worthy, a victim of circumstance, a patsy in life's grand scheme. The other claims I am 'all that is' capable of grandeur with access to unlimited knowledge and power. Spirituality walks the tightrope of the middle path, swaying side to side in an emotional roller coaster of elatory injustices. Spirituality allows for scientific wisdom, whilst also incorporating a belief of faith in a higher divine power, but with the awareness of your connection to the higher power. Spirituality reminds us choice always manifests through you – we always have a choice. In certain cases this will be less apparent than others, but dig a little deeper, remove the topsoil and the fertile ground will reveal itself for the seed to be planted and the fruits of life to be offered for your picking. To experience love we must know what fear is. To see the light we must be enveloped within darkness likewise darkness has no place unless light exists. Both sides must be present and both sides are a gift, because it's the only way you can choose who you are at any given moment. It is from your perspective who, where, why and what life is.

The big silence

Did a Big Bang ever really happen or is it all in our imagination? It was Edwin Hubble (later made famous by the Hubble telescope) who in 1929 discovered the distance between far away galaxies was increasing at an exponential rate. They were hurtling away from each other at faster and faster rates. This was a complete shock to the physics community who, for the most part, had sided with either Einstein's view of a steady state universe or the slowing down of the Big Bang energy, eventually leading to a Big Crunch. Hubble's discovery was the catalyst for the Big Bang theory. It gained momentum decades later, when more observable evidence 'came to light', and appeared to back it up. In simple terms, it is postulated that, if galaxies are currently moving away from each other at an ever increasing rate, then - by running the clock backwards in a linear fashion - you end up with a minuscule point of potentially infinite energy. This has been calculated to be approximately 13.8 billion years ago (for this to occur two bouts of cosmic inflation were required to be added for the computer models to work - or no universe). Note:- the assumption to the connection of linear time.

There are two ways to tell this story. If we take "you" out of the picture we have - out of nothingness an infinitesimally small point formed having an infinitesimally large amount of energy. This energy exploded into existence bringing forth space, time, energy and matter as we know it......damn we're back in the picture again! This primordial expansion – at times faster than light speed - led to the formation of everything without any sign of an initial contraction.

Faster than light speed? I thought this was the universal speed limit! Yes and no according to the Big Bang theory. Special relativity suggests objects close together cannot move faster than the speed of light with respect to one another. Apparently, this does not apply to objects that are extremely far apart. Let me repeat that - the absolute speed of light does not apply to objects that are at extreme distances from our point of reference. The belief is that the space in between the objects (vacuum density) is expanding so much it is causing the objects to fly away from each other at faster than light speeds. Hence, there is not enough time for light to travel back to us. The Big Bang theory breaks a number of fundamental physics principles. "For every action there's an equal and opposite reaction" comes to mind. Where is the primordial contraction to allow for the expansion? What medium did sound travel through in the beginning to create a bang? Who would have heard it? How did thoughts, feelings, emotion and self-awareness all originate from something as insentient as matter? The computer models fail without the inclusion of two bouts of inflation (a speeding up in the early universe at faster than light speeds to account for current observational discrepancies), the inclusion of dark matter, dark energy and more recently dark flow - which ironically, all due to their "darkness", are undetectable - and many, many other tweaks. But hey! Why ruin a good story by letting a few minor issues get in the way? "The universe must be material and out there because it's only common sense. Anyone who thinks otherwise is just plain stupid and, if I shout loud enough and mock them in front of others for laughs, I must be right! My senses would never lie......or would they?"

It is widely accepted that eye witness accounts can be very misleading. In a court of law, to convict someone the evidence must suggest beyond reasonable doubt. This is because a fact cannot exist from all perceivable points of view. An element of doubt always arises no matter what. In the quantum world - from where everything originates - this is known as Heisenberg's uncertainty principle. We can never know where a sub-atomic particle is and, at the same time, how fast it's travelling and in what direction. This is crucial, because it impacts our everyday lives without us even realising it. It is connected to special relativity in our macroscopic world. This is why a fact can only appear as a fact to an observer from their own point of view. It does not make it a fact to someone else. This is very difficult for most people to accept. I will repeat once again - there is no 'the truth' only 'your perceived truth'.

Let's bring 'you' back into the equation......did you ever truly exit? As an observer looking through a telescope, applying the law of opposites across the boundary condition (you), what we are interpreting is the red shift of 'light' signatures emitted by galaxies at the farthest edges of the observable universe. It's the red shift of light that tells us that galaxies are travelling away from each other exponentially. Beyond this point there is not enough time for the light to reach us. Note:- It is only light that is being observed not a galaxy. It is the observer (us) who is deciding it is a galaxy.

We established earlier that the exponential function (Euler's number) appears to be built into the mathematics from our 'spiritual' point of view. It is the observer who creates the outer boundary condition, due to our 'finite' biological nature within an 'infinite' universe. But what happens when we reverse this process and look back in time? Applying the law of opposites to the exponential function we would assume, from our perspective, that the further we looked back in time, the 'slower and slower the universe would recede infinitely'. This is in agreement with Haramein's conclusion that the universe - and everything within the universe - is all interconnected in a non-linear way. Once again, due to the perspective of the finite nature of biology, we would expect to observe the opposite boundary condition - which we do (the cosmic microwave background radiation). This, interestingly, is what you see when your television is not tuned in properly. It exists today (now) in every point in space. Therefore, looking from the perspective of the observer, the Big Bang never happened! No matter the extent of our technological advances, the observer's story always dwells within boundary conditions put there by the observer. This is in total agreement with the most up-to-date research in quantum physics and, when the materialistic bias is eradicated from our current scientific way of thinking, we will look back and ponder why we the human species can be so bloody pedantic!

The universe appears infinite, yet paradoxically a unique finite reality tunnel is constructed in every moment by everyone, with many interfering (overlapping) with each other, creating patterns we each enlighten holographically from our point of view to enact our daily performances. The finite reality tunnels we create, through the stories we tell using our sensory awareness, can be within the four walls of a soundproof room or the Milky Way when gazing up at the stars.

There will always be limits to how far we can see in either direction, and this makes sense because, if your spiritual essence is infinite then the world of experience you create must appear finite. The trick is to not impose self restricting boundaries; to know without doubt the source is infinite and unbounded - to allow anything of your choosing. For you to have the experience of what you choose, boundary conditions will appear which are relative in nature. It really isn't that complicated - we, as a species, just like to make it appear so!

When you are able to see life as an interplay between silence and noise, order and chaos, spirit and objective reality, with you at the centre, then the realisation dawns that it is YOU choosing the perspective to how YOU wish to perceive the experience of YOUR choice. It is you who is the real orchestrator!

CHAPTER 8

My Place in the Universe
(what it all means to me)

The aim up to now was to provide a different perspective to how we commonly see the world. To alter the belief that we are insignificant entities living in a cold harsh environment, fearful of the unknown and perpetually worried of what might happen to ourselves and loved ones in the future. This view of life is depressing, self defeating and can be very draining, but extremely common. Look at it this way - in the west anyone who is interested in television programmes devoted to the universe - our place in it and the nature of reality - is mainly subjected to the same core people voicing their opinion, from their perspective of their specialised field. Time after time the same information, with only the occasional deviation (which I must add is always shrouded in speculation) is put forward. This is not to denigrate the people in question, because their opinion is as equally valid as is anyone else's. It's the broader spectrum of opinions that rarely gets aired. Believe me, when you dig a little deeper you will discover a multitude of varied approaches to the nature of everything. It is only by doing so that you are provided with the scope to satisfy that deepest yearning of who you are and what it's all about. A little information services a closed mind. A myriad opens up the truth.

A spiritual awakening can come about in many different ways. Some experience what is known as the kundalini effect (a radical and very quick transformation), others become aware as a result of near death experiences, whilst people like myself experience a more gradual and prolonged awakening, quite often spawning from a personal tragedy. The end result is always the same. Once you are awakened there is no going back. Not, I believe, that you would want to, but the veil to the bigger picture has been removed.

So, what is this bigger picture? In my experience, I initially became aware that the story I was telling myself, or at least the influences, were very one dimensional. I quite often accepted the authoritative view at face value, and without question. Yes I always had my own opinion, but that opinion was very mainstream. By mainstream I mean heavily influenced by the media and people who I felt were more educated in specialised fields than myself. This one dimensional approach mainly functions from a black or white perspective. We're the goodies, you're the baddies. I'm right, you're wrong. In retrospect it appears childlike. It is a very superficial way of interpreting life, but extremely common. People in power know this and use it to their advantage, why wouldn't they? If you are prepared to do the bidding of another why would the other prevent you. It is not the other taking your power, it is you giving your power away! In today's society when you spiritually awaken your first reaction is OMG!.......WTF!!!

The dark side creates balance

Seriously though, when you awaken what quite often happens is that you come face to face with the dark side - otherwise known as conspiracy theories. This is almost inevitable, because prior to you morphing into your doppelgänger you were more likely to accept information at face value. Life now appears more like a balance beam and by seeing the broader picture you reposition yourself more centrally, but ironically what tends to happen is that you slowly slide into the conspiratorial side at the other extreme. This is a whole new angle to view life from, and there appears to be plenty of evidence to back it up. The story you tell yourself becomes more radical and eye opening and, as human beings, we all love a good thriller.

When I first had my eyes opened I wanted to tell the world and guess what? The world didn't want to know.

I went deeper and deeper into the dark side - seeing the complete opposite to what had been portrayed throughout my lifetime. My world turned upside down. Everywhere I looked I could create a story out of this new information that was now available. The story was gripping and exciting and initially seemed to put the worlds wrongs to rights. Problem was, the majority of people I knew thought I was a bit cuckoo! Although - to be fair - most appreciated what I had just gone through. Over time I began to slide back toward the centre of the balance beam again. The stories I constructed about world events became more balanced and less radical. I managed to get unstuck from the dark side. Many, it would appear, do not. They become addicted to telling the darker version of events, even though they can still see the bigger picture. What basically happened is that they have gone from one extreme to another. It's all a psychological drama!

Become centred

Conspiracy theories aren't bad per se. A conspiracy theory is just a belief that the reported version of events doesn't add up. The mainstream version is quite often embroiled in a monetary power struggle at a higher governmental or national level. Do you really believe that everything you're being told is true? If you answer "yes" to this, I'm gobsmacked you have read so far. I suggest you check the meaning of 'gullible'.

What I am saying is, when you truly become aware you will see both sides of the story. At this point you then have to filter out your bias as best you can, because pure objectivity is impossible from your point of view (this is why you have one). Your bias comes about from your own personal experiences of life and the meaning you have chosen to attribute to them. Having accepted both sides, and removed as much bias as possible, then and only then, can you make the best choice that serves you. Sounds somewhat selfish - it is - because life is self serving! Think about it. If you offer a homeless person money you will inevitably feel good inside. A good deed carried out in the world outside makes you feel good inside. The best choices always come about when you do not affect another in a negative way. What you do to another you do to yourself.....karma! Everyone and everything is a version of you in a different guise. Everything is one at a deeper spiritual level, but the illusion of separation always exists at the human level for the ability to have an experience. Empathy stems from your awareness of your deeper spiritual connectedness and that's why, when you become spiritually awakened, you form a stronger bond to nature and everything in it. The ego's desire for power diminishes because you realise the power is, and always has been, within you. The more forgiving and grateful you become, the more rewarding your experiences become. This operates through the more well known spiritual law of attraction (like attracts like).

By developing an understanding that what you experience on the outside is a holofractographic mental projection, related to the story you're telling yourself, with the choices you are making stemming from a deeper spiritual source, empowers you to grander heights. You are the boundary condition. You exist at the precipice of the inner and outer worlds. In the electromagnetic expression of the world out there opposites attract. In the quantum world of entanglement opposites are linked as one. But when the boundary condition of your inner thoughts and feelings is crossed to the outer world of experience it's like attracts like. Crossing the boundary creates the opposite to the law of opposites......pretty cool? I hope this makes sense, because I believe that when you can see reality functioning in this way, then things which at first appear nonsense begin to make perfect sense.

When your spiritual connectedness has developed, to the point where that point (of view) sits comfortably at the centre of the balance beam, you can appreciate the ebb and flow of life. The beam never remains static......ever. Change is built into the system so life will always involve ups and downs. The uncertainty lies within, but when you 'know without doubt' the outside will reflect as certainty. With so many variables existing, probability usually takes over. It is up to you to know yourself as who you are and apply your new found power. The power lies within you to how you master your mind - to make the best of every situation, whilst always maintaining the faith of a wonderful outcome. When you are able to do this you truly are a mastermind!

It's your novel

The metaphorical Jesus was a mastermind - as were Krishna, Buddha and many others we have heard about through historical stories. They demonstrated their divinity in ways that could only be perceived from the outside as miracles. From their perspective there are no miracles because they understood that life is a miracle and you are a miracle of life. Think of the miracles your body performs everyday just to keep you alive. It's been calculated that your cells correlate up to one trillion functions a second without you giving a second thought! Think of the knowledge we have gained about the universe from living on a small rock at the back end of nowhere. Yes it's all about perspective, but the stories we can tell can be out of this world!

I think it's time for the nitty gritty. Who really are you? The answer of course I believe is based on the law of opposites. At one extreme you are a multidimensional being who can be defined by the mind in many different ways. You could fill a library never mind a book on this topic alone, but, in a nutshell, this is my take. You are a story teller. You are the narrator of the story of your life, but you are also much, much more than that. You are not only the narrator, you are also the narrative and the process of narration. This is another example of the Wholly trinity......the law of opposites based on the power of three.

> "When writing the story of your life don't
> let anyone else hold the pen"

> -Anonymous

From the moment you wake up in the morning, until you go to bed at night, you are embodying the experiences of the story you are telling yourself. The story continues in the dream state, albeit much fuzzier due to a reduction in the ability to focus attention. Only when you are in deep sleep does the narrative cease because from your perspective no time has passed to tell your story. With your battery recharged, upon awakening clocks have been reset for the process to continue, but way down the rabbit hole it is quite the opposite. It is not a continuing process, it is a single act of creation that takes place simultaneously in the one eternal moment of Now. Fundamentally you are recreating your story anew in every single moment. Both perspectives are equally valid although the latter for most seems unimaginable, but this is only due to how you have been conditioned to process information. What most people don't realise is 'information is neutral' and it is you who is deciding what it means, and feeding back through heartfelt emotions to the source, for your next choice to be experienced. The heart is central to this feedback loop.

To me this makes so much sense. It is you who is choosing from an infinity of possibilities through heartfelt feelings linked to mental images. This takes place in the non-local realm (no space and no time) creating an experience which is localised in spacetime co-ordinates holographically via the receiver/transmitter of the brain (and DNA) into what you perceive as reality. The world out there is made up of non-matter and what we perceive as matter, which is really the charged radius of the proton manifesting as light. Let's be honest, if this was easy to comprehend then we would all have worked it out long ago. Everyone of us is at a different rung on the ladder of life for the purpose to experience infinity.

It's time to re-member

We have previously established that each one of us creates our own reality tunnel via spacetime co-ordinates holofractographically. The illusion of solidity comes from the positively charged proton. With the proton related to light (photon), we know from Einstein that at the speed of light there is no time. You create the illusion of time for the purpose of memory to be able to tell your story. Without memory there is no time - without time there is no memory.

Time Is Memory Experienced

-Karen Ferris

You can also link it to change. You require time in order for change to occur and, as we know, the only constant is change. Therefore change, time and memory are all one and the same. Looking at it from this perspective, is it such a gamble to accept the world your senses perceive is a holofractographic story? It strikes fear into some that the world might be illusory, but in reality it is empowering when you embrace it. Embrace this power to tell the story of your dreams.

When the realisation dawns that it is you who is mentally creating space and time and you begin to process life from this perspective, you will take a massive quantum leap in consciousness. As much as your ego tries to invoke the victim complex from previously stored programmes, your new found spiritual awareness overrides this, but only to a point. The ego can only define itself through all of your past experiences and the meaning you have attributed. The ego is in fact the mask you wear to differentiate yourself from everything else. The mask acts as a veil, in which spirit hides behind, until you decide when the moment is right for the big reveal. You could say the ego is a necessary evil for spirit to know itself. But even when you come to know this, on the occasions when you 'react' to situations without being consciously aware, the subconscious programmes still kick in and allow the ego to take control. It takes time to override previous programmes and become responsible for who you really are. This battle between duality and wholeness still ensues and will only cease once you become the master of your mind.

A mastermind is not someone who has a vast amount of knowledge. At a deeper level each one of us has access to this fountain. A mastermind is not even someone who understands complexity. A true mastermind is someone who can demonstrate to themselves, through their actions, the divinity that lies within each and every one of us. I emphasise 'to themselves' because when you align with Wholeness there is no other you need to convince. If you feel the need to convince someone else, the power evaporates. You hold at your source the potential of all the information of the universe. You create the quantum field which you engage with in every single moment of your existence. So, from one perspective, you already are a mastermind and from the opposite you are always seeking the Wholly Grail.

The law of opposites is interwoven throughout all of nature. The reality we experience is a mirror reflection. Everything has its mirror image. For every boom there's a bust. At the universal scale, for our matter based universe to exist, its complementary anti-matter universe must also exist. At the quantum scale every electron has its mirror reflection, the positron, and right at the centre of all this sits biology - with biology composed of the double helix of DNA, which is two strands that are an exact mirror image of each other. We as humans are unique. We get to observe the infinity of the outer world by getting to know the infinity of our inner world.

By contrast it requires just two mirrors to create an infinity of infinities. If the wholeness of spirit, which does not have a boundary, is individuated infinitely as a mirror reflection and each individuation contains within it a second mirror reflection, because the law of opposites still requires an opposite mirror, what we have is infinity looking back at itself infinitely. Wholeness is pure conscious awareness which is impersonal - it must be, as there is nothing else. It's you who exhibits the self-aware personal consciousness.

Wedded bliss

The secret of the hologram is that when you change the information of one aspect the whole hologram changes to reflect the change. From your point of view it is you who constructs the hologram yet paradoxically for a hologram to exist it requires an interference pattern which is all points of view. Think of it this way. All that exists is a composition of every story ever told and it's your divine right to tell your story how you see fit. For better for worse, for richer for poorer, in sickness and in health, as long as you both shall live.

You do so by first deciding exactly what it is you desire to experience outwardly (within the hologram). Remove any doubt you might hold that your desire is unattainable. This is probably the most difficult part as the subconscious programmes, that have conditioned you all of your life to believe who you think you are, need to be deleted. By visualisation (holding in your imagination) and crystallising this mental picture with sensory awareness (image-in-action), create the belief that it is already true (when you ask it is already given) because time, remember, is a mental construct, and let go. You must let go of your desire once you have accepted it. Otherwise you will continue getting what you are actually asking for and that is the wanting. When you are wanting something to happen you will receive just that - the wanting of it. How many people have you heard say "I want to be wealthy". Wealthy people say "I am wealthy". The spiritual wisdom is to know without doubt and know that it is already done for you. The English language is constructed in a negative way and we are conditioned to talk to ourselves from this standpoint. It might provide the answer to the question within psychological circles of why our mindset thinks in the negative approximately 70% of the time.

> "Be the change you want to see in the world"

> -Gandhi

SUMMARY

Throughout the book I have been attempting to piece together all the parts of the puzzle at the fundamental level. Now is not the' time', but the 'moment' to pull it all together. I have shown through scientific evidence - and the spiritual law of opposites - that the world of our perceptions is composed of the electromagnetic field, brought about by the vacuum density Planck scale units which creates the space in between and is the connector of all things. The space in between is the potential difference (voltage) between two points of charge which produces the illusion of the flow of energy (electrical and magnetic). The space in between (vacuum density) is 'potential', which we know of as 'spirit' and at the same time is the creator of the virtual energy/information. Energy and information, we know, are two sides of the same coin. This is what we perceive as matter through our sensory awareness, being an expression of one thing – light at the vacuum density. Creation is the dance between light and darkness – holofractographic black wholes - all bound by love.

We began with the acknowledgement that life is paradoxical, with the solution lying within the higher awareness that it's all about perspective. Life is governed by a holofractographic two way feedback system that is infinite in nature. The question we haven't addressed is why is this the case? Once again complexity is borne out of simplicity. For the one thing to know through experience what it is, a system is required where the one appears to become two and the two become infinite, but behind the veil is 'in all ways' only one. A paradox is inevitable because what appears as two separate entities are always one and the same. For any system to function and come into being requires intelligent design. Therefore the answer to the age old question "does God exist?" must be a YES! This is not a personal God though, but an impersonal one, which I believe is much more acceptable to the scientific, agnostic - and who knows, maybe even the atheist community - don't fret everyone else, a personal God does exist. Take a bow........it is you!

Let me explain......we know that every individual Planck scale unit at the quantum level of the vacuum density carries a single bit of information of light in the form of a photon. Due to the most fundamental law of opposites feedback loop – the one is the many and the many are the one - this paradoxically informs us that each individual photon stores all of the information of the whole universe. You could say every (PSU) is an individual conscious entity - a point of view – with them all collectively being infinitely one. It is all a matter of perspective – on a holofractographic scale. When you from the biological perspective observe (theoretically) 'from above' the ground state of creation – the vacuum density – you could say you are in fact God looking in the mirror at all of itself.

As above so below; The kingdom of heaven is within each and everyone of us all makes perfect sense now. Fundamentally existence is all 'virtually' curled up within itself; reflecting on itself, spinning so fast that it is absolutely still. Life......is a metaphor. This is the Yo(u)niverse Paradox.

This book has been a journey for me into the world of knowingness - inspired by the search for my daughter Robyn. Along the way I have discovered my answers - I hope I have helped you discover some of yours. But to know is only one third of the story. The next chapter is to take action - we must do to become......

"Do or do not, there is no try"

-Yoda

GLOSSARY

Action – to do. In physic's parlance it is angular momentum which is the quantity of rotation of a body, which is the product of its moment of inertia and its angular velocity. In otherwords spin.

Absolute – not subject to any limitation

Black hole – a region of space having a gravitational field so intense that no light (matter and radiation) can escape. The light is pulled into a curved horizon known as the event horizon. At the centre of every black hole is the singularity which is an infinitesimally dense region of space.

Black Whole – similar to a black hole, but spelt "whole" because there is an equilibrium between the information going in and going out (in the form of light) across the event horizon that creates the wholeness of a self-organisIng complete system according to Nassim Haramein's unified field theory.

Coriolis Effect – it is the effect on a rotating body by a force acting perpendicular to the direction of motion causing the spin in each hemisphere to rotate in the opposite direction moving toward the poles. Much like the earths weather system where hurricanes rotate counter clockwise in the northern hemisphere and clockwise in the southern.

Field – in physics terms a field is a physical quantity that has a value for each point in space and time. An example is an electric field emanates from an electric charge throughout the whole of space.

Feedback loop – the constant exchange of information of a system relating to cause and effect.

Fractal – A self similar infinitely repeating pattern across all scales. Fractals are created by a simple repeating process within an ongoing feedback loop.

Hologram – a three dimensional image reproduced from a two dimensional pattern of interference produced by a split coherent beam of radiation (laser).

Holographic principle – the theory suggests the entire universe can be viewed as two-dimensional information stored on the cosmological horizon yet experienced by biology (the observer effect) as three dimensional space.

Metaphysical – of or relating to the transcendent or to a reality beyond what is perceptible to the senses.

Objective world – the world we perceive 'out there' with our senses.

Observer effect – the influence an observer's bias has not only on sub-atomic particles, but experiments have now shown on the macro world of our experience.

Omnipotence – all powerful

Omniscience – all knowing

Omnipresence – everywhere

Paradox – a situation, circumstance or event which the mind cannot resolve.

Photon – see Planck scale unit.

Planck scale unit (PSU) – a discreet quantity of energy proportional in magnitude to the frequency of the radiation it represents. It is also a single photon of light carrying a single bit of information always exhibiting the same discreet amount of angular momentum or action.

Quantum – see Planck scale unit.

Quantum field – see vacuum density.

Quantum theory – often referred to as quantum mechanics or quantum physics explains the behaviour of energy at the atomic and sub-atomic level. It is a description of the microscopic world in terms of probability waves which make up the macroscopic world of our senses.

Singularity – a point at the centre of a black hole or black whole which is infinitely dense.

Spacetime – the concept of time and three dimensional space fused as one in a four dimensional continuum.

Special relativity – it explains how to interpret motion between different inertial frames of reference – that is, objects that are moving at constant speeds relative to each other. It informs us that an observer travelling at light speed would experience no spacial co-ordinates and no time passing.

Subjective world – the inner mental world of personal thoughts and feelings.

Superposition – everything exists everywhere or paradoxically nowhere all at the same time until an observer collapses 'the wave function' into what we perceive as our personal reality tunnel.

Temporal – of or relating to time.

Vacuum density – considered by many to be the bible of physics 'Gravitation' states on page 426 "….present day quantum field theory "gets rid by a renormalisation process" of an energy density in the vacuum that would formerly be infinite if not removed by this renormalisation." In a nutshell if quantum theory as its taught did not tamper with its own conclusions then what we perceive as empty space is in fact infinitely dense just as the holofractographic theory suggests. It is the underlying energy that exists throughout all of space. Also known as the quantum field and the zero point field.

Printed in the United States
By Bookmasters